CLASSIC *f*M

Composers' Notes

Presented by
John Suchet

Written by
Tim Lihoreau

EDITION PETERS

LONDON · FRANKFURT/M · LEIPZIG · NEW YORK
www.editionpeters.com

Peters Edition Limited

Hinrichsen House
10–12 Baches Street
London
N1 6DN

Tel: 020 7553 4000
Fax: 020 7490 4921
email: sales@editionpeters.com
internet: www.editionpeters.com

First published 2006
© Copyright 2006 by Classic FM

ISBN 1-84367-026-7

A catalogue record for this book is
available from the British Library

Cover design by Lynette Williamson

Printed in England by Halstan & Co, Amersham, Bucks.

CONTENTS

Foreword 4

Preface.. 5

The composers:

Vivaldi.. 6

Mussorgsky... 13

Mozart... 21

Debussy... 29

Bach 36

Rossini... 43

Berlioz 49

Verdi 54

Tchaikovsky... 61

Bizet 68

Chopin... 74

Grieg 80

Boccherini... 88

Gershwin 95

Dvořák 102

Haydn 109

Meyerbeer 116

Liszt 123

Schubert 130

Handel.. 136

Massenet... 143

Beethoven 150

Mendelssohn 157

Offenbach 163

Paganini 169

Saint-Saëns... 176

Rachmaninov... 181

The rich list... 188

FOREWORD

Composers' Notes **with Prudential**

At Prudential we believe in bringing the subject of money to life. That's why we've worked with Classic FM to bring you *Composers' Notes*, an in-depth look at the most intriguing financial lives of the great composers.

From the most prudent composer to the truly frivolous, you're sure to find a story here that reflects your own.

Helping you to compose your financial future. It's all part of The Plan from the Pru.

Nick Prettejohn
Chief Executive, Prudential UK

PREFACE

We've all read about artists starving in their garrets, shoulders wrapped against the icy winter, struggling to translate their thoughts into words, musical notes, or brush strokes. So potent and poignant a scene is it, that Puccini composed his best-loved opera around it.

But did it make him any money, or was he a penniless Bohemian too? And what of earlier great composers? We all know what happened to Mozart. He died penniless, his body thrown in a commoners' grave because his widow could not afford a proper funeral. Wrong. It wasn't like that at all.

And Beethoven, who throughout his life wore ragged clothes in need of repair, who frequently borrowed money, and was once arrested on the street as a tramp. Broke? Goodness me, no. More money passed through his hands than you would believe.

We're slightly embarrassed to talk about money in this day and age. You wouldn't ask your colleagues how much they earn. But be honest, you'd love to know. So how much did the great composers earn? When they got the money, did they hang on to it? And who earned the most?

You won't find all that many millionaires in the pages that follow. But just imagine how many of these composers would be rich beyond their dreams if they were alive today. Next time you hear a mobile phone ring to the tune of *Für Elise*, think of the royalty cheque that would have landed on Beethoven's doormat.

John Suchet

VIVALDI'S NOTES

Name:	Antonio Lucio Vivaldi
Nationality:	Italian
Born:	4 March 1678

That's the same year as ... the Popish Plot in England

Died:	28 July 1741

The same year ... that Handel wrote Messiah

Wealth rating:	🜊

Antonio Lucio Vivaldi was born on 4 March 1678 in Venice. His father was first a tailor and then a barber, before going on to become a professional violinist. He was employed at St Mark's, oddly enough under the name "Rossi", the Italian word for red. The fact that Vivaldi's father was employed under this of all names has led many to suggest that perhaps he also sported a shock of red hair like that which would go on to give Vivaldi Junior his nickname – more of which a little later.

As a young child, Vivaldi toured extensively with his father, not only to church festivals but also to opera houses in various Italian towns, where his father would oversee local productions. Later, when Vivaldi became much more famous as a composer than his father had ever been as a violinist, Vivaldi would live with his father and employ him as an in-house copyist for much of his musical output.

At the age of 15, Vivaldi underwent his tonsure – that is, the shaving of his head prior to becoming a priest. His full ordination took place on 23 March 1703, and he soon came to be known as "il prete rosso", or "the red priest", because of his aforementioned shock of red hair.

In September the same year, Vivaldi was also hired by the Ospedale della Pietà in Venice as its violin teacher. The Pietà was, in name, a hospital, but appears to have functioned more as a charity-cum-orphanage-cum-music school for girls. So, from 1703, Vivaldi had two salaries – one from his job as a house priest, or mansionario as it was called, and one from the Pietà. We know the Pietà paid him 60 ducats per annum at first, which would have been more or less comfortable, but nothing breathtaking. The ducat is generally reckoned to be a little more than the value of the English crown of the time, so his salary was the equivalent of slightly less than £2,000. A year later, his Pietà salary was increased to 100 ducats – around £3,200 – when he started to teach different stringed instruments.

In 1706, although he had only been a priest for just three years, he gave up saying mass, and, subsequently, gave up the mansionario's wages, too. Vivaldi complained that a childhood chest complaint, possibly something akin to asthma today, meant that he couldn't see a mass through, and was constantly having to leave the altar. Despite being put on a charge, as it were, for "conduct unbecoming a priest" – namely, refusing to say mass – he was now able to devote himself solely to his music.

It was at this point that Vivaldi's life began a series of ups and downs. He was dropped from the staff of the Pietà in 1709, almost certainly as a result of a cost-cutting exercise. Two years later, he was re-employed on his original salary of 60 ducats. A period of relative stability followed, after which he appears to have had the much-needed break he'd been looking for. In 1716, the Pietà's head of composition left. Vivaldi was in the right place at the right time.

History has been somewhat unfavourable to the outgoing composition maestro of the Pietà, Francesco Gasparini. Vivaldi was given the chance to fill his shoes, the only catch being that he still had to teach violin, but for no extra money. Vivaldi acquiesced to the arrangement and it appears to have paid off. Soon after, Vivaldi's long list of compositions, which he had supplied to fill the hole left by Gasparini, was rewarded with an extra 50 ducats on top of his salary, bringing his earnings per annum to the grand total of 110 ducats, or around £3,500 today.

By now, Vivaldi had also begun to compose operas. He would supplement his income not only by touring to supervise the various productions, but also by selling manuscript versions of the music. As well as operas, Vivaldi began to build a reputation as a composer of concertos. Manuscript copies of these works circulated in many of the fashionable courts, and one place that couldn't seem to get enough Vivaldi concertos was Germany. The composer Johann Sebastian Bach had his own copies and transcribed several of them for the keyboard. Vivaldi is known to have favoured selling manuscript versions of his music over printed versions, and this was solely for financial reasons. With printing, very often the composer had to bear the costs and then sell enough copies to break even. With manuscripts, however, the transcription costs were a fraction of the printing – almost nothing, if he used his father to do the transcription – plus, he could sell each copy for the English equivalent of one guinea each – that's around £100 today.

> ## COMPOSERS' NOTES NOTE
>
> ### *Where is Gloria's twin sister?*
>
> It's a little publicised fact that one of Vivaldi's most iconic works, his setting of the Gloria, was in fact one of two Glorias that he wrote. The other, sadly, is lost.
>
> recommended **1**

In 1718, Vivaldi hit 40. He gave up his teaching post at the Pietà and began to travel. He took one of his operas, *Armida*, to Mantua and proceeded to stay there for a couple of years. This was probably all down to the governer of Mantua, Prince Philip of Hesse-Darmstadt, a well-known supporter of music and musicians at the time. Vivaldi became his music director, with the title Head of Secular Music – presumably his religious intentions were now left firmly behind. By the time he had moved on from the Mantuan court, Vivaldi had several new works under his belt. After a brief return to Venice, he moved on to Rome.

Vivaldi stayed three seasons in Rome, writing music for the carnivals each year. This included several operas and, almost certainly, several works for the influential cardinal, Pietro Ottoboni. By the time he was 45, in 1723, the familiar governing body of the Venice Pietà reared its head once more.

July 1723 saw the red-tape-riddled committee of the Pietà agree to ask Vivaldi to supply them with two concertos per month. It is a sign of Vivaldi's standing as a composer at the time that they had decided, regardless of the fact that he could no longer teach there, that his music meant enough to them to have him send it on by post. Composer in non-residence, if you like. Vivaldi jumped at the offer – he even negotiated with the Pietà that they, not he, would pay the postage. Between the years 1723 and 1729, Vivaldi supplied the Pietà with 140 concertos, at a price of one sequin each. The sequin was the unit of currency in 18th-century Italy. One sequin was worth about the same as one ducat, so this was the equivalent of around about £4,480 today.

One set of concertos he supplied was called *Il cimento dell'armonia e dell'inventione – The battle between harmony and invention.* The battle is meant to be between the regular, restrictive rules of harmony and the free, limitless imagination of sheer invention. The first four of these concertos are now better known as *The Four Seasons.* At the going rate for the Pietà at the time – one sequin per concerto – that means *The Four Seasons* netted Vivaldi just four sequins – or around £130 today. **recommended 4**

It was around this time that Vivaldi became involved on some level with Anna Giro, an alto singer. She was to be found on many Italian opera stages in her day, almost always accompanied by her sister, Paolina, as her chaperone. Vivaldi became, in one way or another, quite attached to Anna, to the point of favouring her over allegedly more able singers. He was even said to have watered down some of his arias to make them more easily performable by Giro. Inevitably, gossip began to build up around the relationship. Giro and Vivaldi were lovers, said some. Giro and Vivaldi *and* Paolino were lovers, said others. In the end, Vivaldi had to address the rumours head on, in print, for fear that he would be ruined. Observers looking back now are divided as to whether anything was actually going on.

Somewhere between the ages of 48 and 50, Vivaldi returned to Venice but not to the Pietà. Instead, his reputation ever growing, he went to the small theatre of San Angelo. Here, he was not only invited to compose but also was allowed to act as entrepreneur and impresario. During this period of his life, he was probably earning the most he would ever earn. Because of his many different incomes, quite how much is hard to calculate. One contemporary source did try to estimate his wealth – and we'll come on to that soon.

By now, Vivaldi was also able to travel more or less as he pleased and, as a result, was able to find himself many a useful patron. Indeed, in 1728, Vivaldi met Charles VI and, with excellent entrepreneurial timing, immediately dedicated a set of concertos to him. Vivaldi called them "La Cetra" ("The Lyre"). The result was apparently not only a substantial fee, but also a complimentary gold chain and medallion.

Vivaldi spent most of the years 1729 to 1733 travelling, visiting places like Vienna and Prague, staging his operas and showcasing his concertos. After 1733, he based himself back in Venice, largely to premiere his operas. Occasionally, he would venture to Ancona, Verona and Ferrara to oversee first nights. From 1734 onwards, much of Vivaldi's correspondence sees him labelled Maestro di Capella to the Duke of Tuscany, although this was probably not a salaried role. Then, in 1735, he was reappointed, once again, at the Venice Pietà. This time, the governing body wanted him permanently in the building and they tried to take a much harder line on his travelling. Vivaldi resisted and, as a result, his numerous absences meant he lost the Pietà job, yet again, three years later. Even then, he did maintain links with the Pietà and continued to sell them works on an ad hoc basis, for many years. The Pietà appears to have been in Vivaldi's blood.

Vivaldi spent much of 1739 in Ferrara, again staging his operas. He had agreed to have three presented, one during each carnival season for the next three years. Unfortunately, the impresario in Vivaldi appears to have gotten the better of the composer. A series of financial and production wrangles ended with him barred from the city of Ferrara by the Archbishop, Cardinal Ruffo. As a result, only the first of the three planned operas was staged, and this without Vivaldi's input. It can have been little comfort to the composer that it may have been his lack of directorial input which led to what was, at best, an unsuccessful opera. At worst, it appears to have been a shambolic performance. The Ferrara authorities subsequently refused to stage the other two operas.

Back in Venice in 1739, Vivaldi's reputation wasn't good. He still had his trading arrangement with the Pietà, and they purchased some 20 concertos from him just a year later. In 1740, probably on the advice of Anna Giro, he travelled to Vienna, hoping to stage at least two of his operas at the city's Kärntnertortheater. By the time he arrived, the death of Charles VI meant that all theatres had been closed for the entire carnival season. No theatres meant no operas, and no operas was bad news for Vivaldi. He stayed on in Vienna well into 1741. It was around this time that he became ill with what was described as "internal inflammation". He managed to sell a number of concertos to a local count, but it was to prove inconsequential. By 28 July, he was dead, and buried in a pauper's grave at the Hospital Burial Ground. The funeral expenses came to around 20 ducats, more or less an equal class of funeral as Wolfgang Amadeus Mozart's, 50 years later.

At this point, a Venetian magazine, the *Commemoriali Gradenigo*, attempted to estimate the composer's income. It stated that the composer *"who once earned 50,000 ducats died in poverty through his own prodigality"*. If that is anywhere near an accurate estimate, it would mean that, during the course of his life, Vivaldi was thought to have let the equivalent of around £1.6 million slip through his fingers. Based on what we know through his letters, I think this was possibly folklore.

So Vivaldi was rich enough, possibly extremely rich, during his lifetime, but he died the classic composer-pauper.

RECOMMENDED LISTENING

 GLORIA IN D MAJOR
The Sixteen/Orchestra of Harmony and Invention/ Harry Christophers

 "NULLA IN MUNDO PAX SINCERA" ("THERE IS NO PEACE IN THE WORLD") FROM MOTET IN E MAJOR RV630
Anke Herrmann/Academia Montis Regalis/ Alessandro de Marchi

 VIOLIN CONCERTO IN E MINOR RV277 "IL FAVORITO"
Viktoria Mullova/Il Giardino Armonico/Giovanni Antonini

 ***THE FOUR SEASONS* OP. 8**
Nigel Kennedy/Berlin Philharmonic Orchestra

 CONCERTO IN G MAJOR FOR TWO MANDOLINS RV532
Ugo Orlandi/Dorina Frati/I Solisti Veneti/Claudio Scimone

MUSSORGSKY'S NOTES

Name: Modest Petrovich Mussorgsky

Nationality: Russian

Born: 21 March 1839
That's the same year that ... Poe wrote The Fall of the House of Usher

Died: 28 March 1881
The same year that ... Picasso was born

Wealth rating: 💷

Modest Petrovich Mussorgsky was born in the small Russian province of Karevo, some 1,000 kilometres north-east of Moscow, on 21 March 1839. His family were fairly wealthy by local standards and Mussorgsky grew up in a house well accustomed to more than a dozen servants. He was the second of two surviving sons and was taught piano very early on by his mother. By all accounts, he was a natural pianist and, when he was only nine, he was able to astound a private audience with a rendition of a John Field piano concerto.

In addition to this early musical tuition, Mussorgsky himself would always say that his grandmother had schooled him – in the art of Russian folk and fairytales. The influence of his mother's music and his grandmother's stories would never leave him.

The family moved to St Petersburg in 1849 where, just three years later, Mussorgsky entered the Cadet School of the Imperial Guards, along with his brother. There was one important difference in their cadetships, though. His brother, Filaret, was the first born and, as a result would inherit *all* the family land and wealth. For him, the cadetship was a temporary affair. Modest, as the second son, would inherit nothing, and was expected to pursue a lifetime's career in the military. For him, the heavy-drinking, womanising Imperial Guards were meant to be for good.

Four years later, at the age of just 16, Mussorgsky entered the Preobrazhensky regiment of the Imperial Guard. On the side, though, he was delighting his new army friends with his exquisite piano playing. It was also around this time that he tried writing his first opera, despite the fact that he'd not had a single moment of formal composition training.

In 1857, he fell in with the composers César Cui and Mily Balakirev. Balakirev, in particular, was considered an emerging, influential composer and he was soon persuaded to give Mussorgsky the composition lessons he needed – paid for by Mussorgsky's mother. She installed a piano in her son's St Petersburg apartment, so that he could keep up his practice.

A year later, the first signs of a nervous disorder began to show in Mussorgsky. Partly brought on by his sensitive nature, partly by his initiation into the Preobrazhensky's heavy drinking, it led to him resigning from his army commission. He was, at this point, still a landed proprietor of the family estates back in Karevo, so financially this was not yet disastrous. He made his first trip to Moscow, the feel and atmosphere of which he loved. He also wrote his first real piece, the Scherzo in B flat, at the request of the conductor Rubinstein. It gained him no money whatsoever, but the Russian Music Society did bear all the costs of its first performance in 1860, conducted by Rubinstein himself. **recommended 1**

At this point, Mussorgsky could have been forgiven for thinking the future looked rosy. He'd had his first piece played, and he had lots of plans for many more. Just one year later, though, came the emancipation of the serfs in Russia. As part of new legislation, serfs were to be freed and set up with land, although this would still belong to both the commune and the landlords. Mussorgsky was forced home to Karevo and spent two years there, helping his brother manage the transfer of the land. He himself retained some small landlord's control over a part of it, but he would never reap much of the financial harvest.

At the time, the Mussorgskys owned around 27,000 acres of land, spread over some 18 villages and a total population of approximately 400 people. His brother Filaret did most of the arduous financial negotiations with the serfs while Mussorgsky remained more detached. It is said that he often took an old-fashioned, aristocratic approach to money – it wasn't to be talked about if at all possible and, certainly, he would never divulge if he was short.

He spent time with his friends, the Shilovsky family, living under their hospitality at their Glebovo estate near St Petersburg. This allowed him to ignore money and think about composing. Not for long, though. As any income from his minor part in the Karevo estate continued to dwindle, he was forced to take a job – in the Imperial Civil Service. Initially, he became a collegiate secretary in the Central Engineering Authority and later an assistant chief of the Barracks Division. It allowed him some limited time to work on his opera *Salammbô*, which he was destined never to finish.

In 1863, Mussorgsky joined a commune. Dispel all images of hippies and VW camper vans, though – Mussorgsky's commune was a St Petersburg apartment which he shared with five other people, but they called it a commune in the spirit of the Russia of the time. It was here that he started really to compose in earnest and it seems that, musically at least, he was just beginning to find his feet. A year later, Mussorgsky's mother died and he sank into his first bout of dipsomania or alcoholism. His brother's wife persuaded him to come and live with them, which Mussorgsky did for the next three years. Then he was promoted to assistant head clerk at his office and things appeared, once again, to be looking up.

It was short lived, however. A year later, in 1867, he was dismissed from his job in a round of civil service downsizing, and he once again began to run into financial difficulties. Balakirev and his composing friends wrote to him, offering money, but Mussorsgsky's honest and decent old-fashioned attitude prevented him from accepting it.

"In the present situation," he wrote, *"I regard myself as not justified in alarming my friends. My means have shrunk, this is true, but not so far as to deprive me of any possibility of an autonomous existence. I implore you to be calm on my account and to reassure all those dear to me."*

Ironically, it was around now that he wrote one of his most celebrated works. His letters are full of what he referred to as *"my witches"* piece. Unfortunately, his mentor Balakirev hated the new work, something which depressed Mussorgsky far more than could any money problems. Balakirev was meant to have programmed it in one of his concerts but, when he received the score, he refused it, upsetting Mussorgsky immensely. Thankfully, it is one of his most loved works today. It became *A Night on the Bare Mountain.* **recommended 2**

In the autumn of 1868, Mussorgsky moved in with another of his friends, the Opochinin family, relishing the free board, free lodgings and free time to compose – he was working on another new opera. In December, he managed to gain another job, again with the civil service. He was assistant chief in the Forestry Commission, a job for which he was paid around 450 roubles a year – that's probably the equivalent of around £9,000 today. He would keep the job for the next ten years.

Over the course of the next year, he managed to spend time on his new opera, *Boris Godunov*, but in 1871 the completed work was rejected by the Mariinsky Theatre. The reason they gave? There was no female prima-donna role, and, therefore, no big box-office pull. Mussorgsky immediately set about reworking it, going on to make even more changes than those demanded by the Mariinsky Theatre. Also, that year, he moved in with Rimsky-Korsakov, an arrangement thought to be one of the few, perhaps only, times that two great composers have lived together. How, though, did the two composers manage not to infuriate each other with their respective music? Rimsky-Korsakov reveals how in his writings:

"How could we help being in each other's way?" he wrote. *"Well, mornings till noon, Mussorgsky used the piano, and I did copying or orchestration. By noon, he would go to his civil service duties, leaving the piano at my disposal. We accomplished a good deal. He orchestrated {part of}* Boris Godunov, *I finished my* Maid of Pskov*!"*

He doesn't say who used the bathroom first on a morning. In any case, the house-share was short lived – around a year or so – at which point Rimsky-Korsakov went off to get married.

In 1874, the Mariinsky Theater finally mounted a full production of *Boris Godunov.* **recommended 3** Mussorgsky's fee was a mere 125 roubles per performance – and he only got the full fee if the opera played to a full house. In all, there were 21 performances in Mussorgsky's lifetime, realising a grand total of 1,600 roubles. Russia appears to have undervalued its native composer in comparison to, say, the Italian composer Verdi. When in 1862 the Russian Imperial Theatre premiered *La forza del destino*, they paid Verdi around 11,000 roubles.

It was also in 1874 that Mussorgsky went to visit a retrospective of the work of an artist colleague, Viktor Hartmann. Just a year earlier, the composer had been grief-stricken at the sudden death of this friend and the exhibition of his pictures had a massive effect on him. Mussorgsky's drinking was massively increasing, and so his emotional state was already incredibly up and down. It's said he rushed home from the exhibition, on 2 June that year, and by 22 June had finished his new work – simply entitled *Pictures at an Exhibition.* **recommended 4** and **recommended 5**

By 1875, things weren't looking too good for Mussorgsky. Rather ominously, he was working on the piece *Songs and Dances of Death* which he originally called simply *She* (due to the fact that the Russian word for death is feminine – Ona). Friends tried to interest the publishers Jurgenson in *She* but it came to nothing.

Also, in 1875, with several months' rent in arrears, he decided he could no longer afford his own lodgings so moved out to live at the house – and the expense – of a friend, one Pavel Naumov.

A year later, records show that he even sent a letter to the tenants of his small share of the land at Karevo, asking them to send *"as much money as possible"* from the amount he was due – as well as inquiring how the farming arrangements were proceeding. There's no evidence to suggest that his tenants – the Morozovs – ever sent any money at all.

In 1878, at the age of 39, Mussorgsky got a glimmer of good news – he was promoted to the position of collegiate counsellor at work. His salary was raised accordingly to 1,200 roubles per year – only around £13,000 today. However, his drinking continued to jeopardise his job, although a friend of a friend, working

---

COMPOSERS' NOTES NOTE

Blatant Exhibitionism

It took the work of three composers to make *Pictures at an Exhibition* a hit. The score bears the handwritten inscription *"For Publication"* on the front and yet Mussorgsky's sometime publisher, Bessel and Co, neither paid for nor published it in his lifetime. When Bessel *did* acquire the rights, for no fee, after Mussorgsky's death, they asked Rimsky-Korsakov to re-edit it, which he did. Even then, it remained just a pleasant and largely unknown piano suite until 1922. That was the year that the composer Maurice Ravel lighted upon it and re-scored it, this time for full orchestra. From that point onwards, it became an absolute staple of the concert repertoire and still is today. The only problem – Mussorgsky, of course, didn't get a single rouble for it.

---

in the Department of Government Control, managed to have Mussorgsky transferred into his department, under his wing.

This position required little or no work, and allowed the composer to concentrate on the piece he was still writing at the time, the opera *Sorochinsky Fair.* (recommended **6**)

By 1879, the "fake" job in Government Control came to an end and, with it, any financial support for Mussorgsky whatsoever. Seeing his situation, his friends clubbed together to provide him with an ongoing monthly pension of around 180 roubles – around £1,000. A year later, out of the blue, he was offered a concert tour with the alto singer Darya Leonova. They toured 12 provincial towns, giving several concerts in each. Mussorgsky was both accompanist and soloist, giving him the chance to play piano arrangements of his own works. He hoped to clear 1,000 roubles pure profit. Halfway through the tour, though, he wrote: *"The receipts are good, although less than we expected."* Eventually he came out of the whole tour with next to nothing.

Back in St Petersburg, both the accompanying, and unfortunately the drinking, continued and neither were doing him any good. Accompanying just didn't pay much at all – very often, he was forced to accept some gigs where payment was purely the honour of playing.

Remarkably, though, he was still composing. In late November 1880, excerpts from his still as yet unfinished opera, *Khovanshchina*, were performed under Rimsky-Korsakov at the St Petersburg Free Music School. As the concert date approached, Mussorgsky was nowhere to be found. Rimsky-Korsakov, with only a piano score in his possession, was forced to quickly orchestrate the excerpts himself. Mussorgsky turned up on the night of the concert, and, when pulled embarrassed from his seat to take the applause, said how astonished he was that Rimsky-Korsakov had orchestrated them exactly as he had intended to himself! (recommended **7**)

In 1881, Mussorgsky's health went from bad to worse. He was diagnosed as suffering from alcoholic epilepsy, and he eventually died on 28 March 1881, seven days after his 42nd birthday. He did have a will drawn up but it left precious little beyond a few personal effects.

After his death, Rimsky-Korsakov took Mussorgsky's music and set about a vast programme of reshaping and "correcting", cutting and rescoring – even adding new music and moving scenes. Years later, many of Mussorgsky's original plans were recognised for what they were and lots of his original thoughts restored.

RECOMMENDED LISTENING

 SCHERZO IN B FLAT
Berlin Philharmonic Orchestra/Claudio Abbado

 A NIGHT ON THE BARE MOUNTAIN
Royal Liverpool Philharmonic Orchestra/Sir Charles Mackerras

 "ORCHESTRAL SYNTHESIS" FROM *BORIS GODUNOV*
Cleveland Symphony Orchestra/Oliver Knussen

 ***PICTURES AT AN EXHIBITION*, ORIGINAL PIANO VERSION**
Evgeny Kissin

 ***PICTURES AT AN EXHIBITION*, ORCHESTRAL VERSION**
Philharmonia Orchestra/Riccardo Muti

 "HOPAK" FROM *SOROCHINSKY FAIR*
Vienna Philharmonic Orchestra/Valery Gergiev

 "DANCE OF THE PERSIAN SLAVE GIRLS" FROM *KHOVANSHCHINA*
Berlin Philharmonic/Prague Philharmonic Choir/Claudio Abbado

MOZART'S NOTES

Name:	Johannes Chrysostomus Wolfgangus Theophilus Mozart
Nationality:	Austrian
Born:	27 January 1756

That's the same year that ... the Seven Years War commenced

Died:	5 December 1791

The same year that ... Samuel Morse was born

Wealth rating:	😊😊

Johannes Chrysostomus Wolfgangus Theophilus Mozart was born at around 8am on 27 January 1756, at No. 9 Getreidegasse, in the centre of the Austrian town of Salzburg. Mozart's father, Leopold, a composer and musician himself, would no doubt have been anxious at Mozart's birth, given that his wife, Maria Anna, had been in labour seven times before and yet the couple only had one surviving child.

As is now fairly well known, Mozart had precious little boyhood. The years 1761 and 1762 appear to have been his only true juvenile years. He was already very musical, as was his sister, who he nicknamed Nannerl: she was four years older than him. With his dad being a well-regarded violinist, this was always going to be a music-centred house. When little Mozart mastered a tricky piano piece by the composer Wagenseil in less than half an hour, it was probably clear to father Leopold that he had something rather special on his hands. By the age of six, Mozart was already "on the road", being furiously toured by his ambitious father, in the hope of recognition for his boy wonder. Initially, they toured with Nannerl to Munich and to Vienna. In Munich, Mozart played in front of the Elector Maximilian Joseph. In Vienna, he played for the Viennese court – which was then the heart of the

"Holy Roman Empire of German Nations", as it was officially known. For a boy of six to play there was just unheard of. The year 1762 also saw the first of many bouts of illness for Mozart, with the young lad bedridden by rheumatic fever.

In 1763, with Mozart was still only seven, Leopold took the family on tour again. By the time Mozart came back to Salzburg, he would be just ten. He'd have played to Goethe in Frankfurt; for Louis XV in Paris; but, perhaps most significantly of all in 1764, in Paris, he published his first composition, his opus 1: a violin sonata. ❰recommended **1**❱

The Mozarts also visited London. When they arrived, Mozart was just eight, going on nine. He and the family stayed in Covent Garden, then Soho, and eventually Chelsea – which was, in those days, not in but *near* London, and was almost all fields. When they met George III, he apparently tested Mozart by putting various pieces of music in front of him and asking him to play them straight off. Of course, Mozart easily did this, impressing the king, by all accounts. London society was keen to see the young prodigy – tickets for a concert to hear Mozart cost six guineas.

Mozart left England after a couple of nights in Canterbury – with time out to go to the races, apparently – before going on to The Hague, where he performed his first solo concert – mainly because the rest of his family had fallen ill. This was a significant event for the young composer.

From 1766 to 1771 – from the ages of 10 to 15 – Mozart was pretty much an itinerant musician. He had no regular income and so was dependant on his travels and his reputation for his next hot meal. He had already written around 14 symphonies before he was given his first (unpaid) job in 1769. Eventually, he landed his first proper salary as concert master for the Bishop of Salzburg. His father had been working for the bishop for years, and no doubt it was a good word as well as a good reputation that led to his first regular employment. Mozart "celebrated" by immediately leaving for Milan to spend a couple of months on paid leave. It was here he met a male soprano called Venanzio Rauzzini, for whom he wrote *Exsultate, jubilate.* **recommended** **2**

In 1778, aged 22, Mozart arrived in Paris, this time touring with his mother. But while he was there, his mother died. He gradually broke the bad news to his father in his letters, before returning to Salzburg a year later.

By this time, he had added the role of court organist to his duties, giving the 23-year-old significantly more money. His freelance earning power was also high at that time too. For example, in Mannheim, he provided a local nobleman, Baron von Gemmingen, with a number of small pieces, for which he was paid three Louis d'Or – valuable gold pieces from the time. To put one Louis d'Or in context, the expenses of most of 1779, including journeys, food and lodgings, came to a grand total of four Louis d'Ors. Three for just one commission makes you realise Mozart's earning potential.

Mozart received an opera commission from Munich in 1780 – the opera would eventually become *Idomeneo* – and travelled there to supervise the premiere. By 1781, with *Idomeneo* finished, Mozart is ordered – yes, *ordered* – back from Munich by the bishop. Not, however, to Salzburg, but to Vienna, where the bishop happened to be staying. He duly arrived and played, as requested, for the bishop at his Viennese social events. Mozart, however, was far from happy. He had been made to sit with the servants, so remonstrated with the bishop's second in command over his treatment, resigning on the spot before he could be sacked. This was the now infamous occasion which resulted in Mozart being kicked up the backside by the bishop's no. 2. Problematically, he now had no job, no money and no place to stay.

Mozart began lodging with old family friends, the Webers. In earlier times, he had once had a bit of thing for Aloysia Weber, but this was all in the past. This time, however, he fell for Aloysia's sister, Constanze, and they were soon married.

In 1782, Mozart's opera *The Abduction from the Harem* was premiered at Vienna's Burgtheater. By now, Mozart was probably the happiest he would ever be – he had a new wife, a grand new flat in Vienna's Domgasse where they loved to throw parties, and new works were coming thick and fast.

In 1785, the 29-year-old Mozart joined the Freemasons – the Beneficence Lodge – and also produced what has become his most enduring piano concerto of all, No. 21. **recommended 4** The same year, he earned 559 gulden from one concert at the Salzburg's Burgtheater. He sold six quartets, dedicated to Haydn, to his publisher Artaria, for 450 gulden. His father Leopold wrote in his letters: *"I think that, if he doesn't have any debts to pay, he could deposit 2,000 gulden in the bank!"* That's the equivalent of more than £50,000 today.

Mozart spent 1786 performing and conducting as much as possible and generally "raising awareness". He had a baby boy by now, too – Karl Thomas. His piano-concerto count was by now up to 24 and yet, amazingly in the middle of all this, he found time to write an opera, *The Marriage of Figaro*, the first of his collaborations with a rather saucy young chap called Lorenzo da Ponte. The new opera earned him 450 gulden, the equivalent of around £11,000 today. **recommended 5**

By 1787, aged 31, *The Marriage of Figaro* had proved to be a big hit in Prague, leading directly to a commission for his next opera, *Don Giovanni*, another Da Ponte partnership. By now, Mozart's father had died, the impact of which really can't be overstated. This was the man who had, some would say, enveloped Mozart almost all his life. As a child, Leopold was sometimes the only company Mozart had for months on end.

Nevertheless, great music continued to pour out of him. *Eine kleine Nachtmusik* saw out 1787, and then, in 1788, he produced three of his greatest symphonies. No. 39, the much-loved No. 40, and the simply stunning No. 41, later nicknamed the "Jupiter" Symphony. Unfortunately, *Don Giovanni* didn't go down quite so well in Vienna as it did in Prague. It failed at the box office in 1788, leaving the still-freelance Mozart in a bit of a financial spot. The year of revolution, 1789, found Mozart back on tour, then touting for work. His big composition of the year was written for his friend, Mr Stadler, a clarinettist at the Viennese Court: this was his Clarinet Quintet. **recommended 6**

Mozart was now not in great shape, financially. For the last few years, his funding had been touch-and-go. That's not to say money wasn't coming in – it was, and, occasionally, lots of it: but it was also going out pretty fast, too. Just before he wrote *Don Giovanni*, he was forced to move the family out of the expensive Domgasse apartment to a cheaper, smaller one in the less salubrious Landstrasse. When his dad had died, he had actually needed the 1,000 florins that came in his will. By 1789, the world's favourite composer was reduced to writing begging letters to friends. He borrowed from his fellow masons, from acquaintances, from previous patrons. As a result, the physical legacy of Mozart – that is, what he actually left us, on paper – includes not only some of the finest works but also begging letters like this one:

"I'm taking the liberty of writing to you, with no airs and graces, to ask a favour. Can you lend me 100 florins . . . just till 20 May – that's when I get paid, and I'll be able to give you it back."

...or this one...

". . . if you could possibly lend me around one or two thousand florins . . . over one or two years, and at a suitable rate of interest, you'd really be doing me a favour . . ."

. . . and even the one where he asks the lender not to tell, so as not to spoil his chances of a job . . .

"Stick with me . . . as much as you can . . . You can imagine . . . how my present circumstances would ruin my chances at court, if anyone found out."

It's sad to think these desperate begging letters come from the same pen that wrote the opera *Così fan tutte*. `recommended 7` Although he had been promised 900 gulden for the opera, only 450 gulden came in. A letter from 1790 shows Mozart telling his wife Constanze to arrange another loan of 1,000 gulden, which she presumably did.

At the age of 34, time was running out for Mozart. By the end of the year, 1791, he would be dead. Everything he wrote from this point on became his *ultimate* works. But what a set of works: the piano concerto no. 27, for example – for which the publisher Artaria paid him 108 florins – and *The Magic Flute*, an opera crammed full of Masonic symbols and references. `recommended 8` Mozart was able to sell handwritten copies of the opera for 100 gulden each.

During this final year, Mozart visited his wife at Baden, where she was enjoying a local cure, and also found time to help out a family friend, Anton Stoll. Stoll was a Baden schoolteacher who ran the music at the Parish Church. As well as this, he had helped the Mozarts sort out all the domestic arrangements for their visit – hired them lodgings, etc – and so Mozart paid back the favour in the only way he could: in music. On 17 June 1791, he penned a little motet for Stoll's choir, setting the words of the *Ave verum corpus*, to be sung on the feast of Corpus Christi. `recommended 9`

Back in Vienna, the dark figure of Count von Walsegg reared his head. Walsegg's wife had died aged only 20 and he had been beside himself with grief. Walsegg asked Mozart for a requiem, something that would mean she would always be remembered. The work was, though, to be passed off as Walsegg's own. Mozart, of course, needed the cash, and so accepted immediately. Before he could start on it, he tripped off to Prague for the coronation celebrations of the new emperor, Leopold II. His new opera, *La clemenza di Tito*, was premiered at the National Theatre. When he got back to Vienna, in September, Mozart finished off *The Magic Flute* and immediately busied himself with the premiere.

He also set to work on the clarinet concerto recommended **10**, before remembering his commitment to Walsegg.

He was now seriously overworking, and his health and state of mind began to take a tumble. He began to suffer from delusions – one was that he was being poisoned, which would start all manner of trouble when he was gone. In fact, he became generally unwell. By October, Constanze had gone back to Baden, and her absence depressed him further. The Viennese weather – sleet, rain, snow – was all pretty bad for his failing health. He suffered from abdominal pains and rheumatic fever and, in his sad state, uttered the now famous phrase: *"I am writing this requiem for myself!"*

Eventually, at the end of October, Constanze returned, and Mozart seemed to pick up, though he didn't get out much. In fact, on 20 November, he took to his bed, feeling particularly awful. His doctors were called in and, by early days of December, he had rallied. He was still full of doom and gloom though – enough of a pessimist, in fact, to gather a bunch of musicians round his bed to practise the requiem, just in case. He even gave his composition pupil, Süssmayr, some details on how to complete it when he was dead. On 4 December, the doctor was called out again and he found Mozart burning up. The composer lapsed into unconsciousness that night. On the morning of 5 December 1791, at around 12.55am, he died. Constanze wept, uncontrollably, by his corpse and refused to leave his side.

Constanze was advised that because of her financial position, she should elect for what was called "a third-class funeral". The cost of this was four florins and 36 krona, as well as four florins and 20 krona for the church. Added to this, the wagon that took Mozart's corpse from Vienna's Rauhensteingasse to St Stephen's Cathedral and then on to St Marx's cemetery cost three gulden. No one knows the final resting place. Every now and then, some poor cadaver is DNA-tested but, so far, he hasn't been found.

RECOMMENDED LISTENING

 VIOLIN SONATA – MOZART'S OPUS 1
Rachel Podger/Gary Cooper

 EXSULTATE, JUBILATE
Cecilia Bartoli/Vienna Chamber Orchestra/György
Fischer

 CORONATION MASS
English Concert/English Concerto Choir and
soloists/ Trevor Pinnock

 PIANO CONCERTO NO. 21
Murray Perahia/Chamber Orchestra of Europe

 "SULL'ARIA" FROM *THE MARRIAGE OF
FIGARO*
Véronique Gens/Patrizia Ciofi/Concerto Cologne/
René Jacobs

 CLARINET QUINTET IN A
Thea King/Gabrieli String Quartet

 **"SOAVE SIA'IL VENTO" FROM** *COSÌ FAN
TUTTE*
Renée Fleming/Anne Sofie von Otter/Michele
Pertusi/Chamber Orchestra of Europe/Sir Georg
Solti

 "THE BIRDCATCHER'S ARIA" FROM *THE
MAGIC FLUTE*
Bryn Terfel/Metropolitan Opera Orchestra/James
Levine

 AVE VERUM CORPUS
Choir of Trinity College, Cambridge/Richard
Marlow

 CLARINET CONCERTO IN A
Sabine Meyer/Berlin Philharmonic Orchestra/
Claudio Abbado

DEBUSSY'S NOTES

Name: Achille-Claude Debussy

Nationality: French

Born: 22 August 1862
That's the same year that ... Victor Hugo wrote Les Misérables

Died: 25 March 1918
The same year that ... Max Planck introduced his "Quantum Theory"

Wealth rating: £

Achille-Claude Debussy, to give him his original name, was born on 22 August 1862 in Saint-Germain-en-Laye, to Victorine and Manuel Debussy. At the time, his father ran a small china shop and the family were by no means wealthy. When Debussy was five, the family moved to Paris and, with the financial help of both friends and the French authorities, he entered the Paris Conservatoire. He was ten years old and studying with some of the finest musical minds France had to offer at the time. His piano teacher, Antoine Marmontel, was particularly legendary, although it is said Debussy would often frustrate him by refusing to obey the rules of harmony on the piano. *"The only rule is my ear!"* was his mantra.

From a very early age, Debussy apparently exhibited a taste for the finer things in life. He had a predilection for delicate sweets and fine pastries. It's said there was a patisserie near the conservatoire into which the music students would pour after a day's lessons. Where others gorged themselves on quantities of croissants or pain au chocolat, Debussy would instead buy only the most expensive, delicate, fine bonbons. In fact, it was something that would stay with him all his life – both his sweet tooth and his tendency to extravagance.

At the age of 18, an important person entered Debussy's life. Nadezhda von Meck is chiefly remembered today as the patron of Tchaikovsky, to whom she gave an allowance for many years. It is less well known that she also engaged the teenage Debussy for three consecutive summers to be her in-house pianist. In Russia, he taught her children how to play the piano, and he travelled with her to Switzerland and Italy. In return he received a small fee and board and lodgings – not a bad arrangement for a student. As a result, there exists an intriguing series of letters from von Meck to Tchaikovsky on the subject of Debussy – or, as she called him, *"my little Frenchman!"*

When he was 21, Debussy entered the composition prize that all French composers coveted – the Prix de Rome. He came second and vowed to have nothing to do with the prize ever again. A year later, though, he entered again and this time he won. The prize's importance was largely prestige, although it did come with a small amount of cash and what was meant to be two years of composer paradise: staying at the Medici Villa in Rome. Debussy, however, professed to hate every minute of his stay in Rome and often kept himself apart from his fellow composers in the villa.

COMPOSERS' NOTES NOTE

Magical fire music

Music was often Debussy's secret weapon in these troubled times. In fact, when you see a piece of his called *"Evenings lit up by the glowing of coal"* don't be fooled into thinking this is just an evocative, romantic title. It was actually written as payment and thank you to a friend who had donated him a much needed bag of coal to keep him warm in his garret flat.

Back in Paris by 1887, it's fair to say that Debussy's bohemian years began in earnest. No longer did he have the cushion of conservatoire support and yet his fine tastes had not ceased.

He managed, somehow, to visit Bayreuth twice to hear Wagner's operas. He also managed to stray into the great Paris Exposition in 1889, where he was completely enchanted by the sound of the Javanese gamelan.

The same year as he witnessed the Paris Exposition, Debussy also wrote the *Petite Suite*. It was championed by a friend of Debussy's, Jacques Durand – son of a famous publisher. At the first performance, as Durand wrote at the time, *"the reception was kind but . . . I was well aware that we had not broken through"*. Now, of course, the piece is treasured. **(recommended 1)**

Throughout these bohemian times, Debussy's behaviour began to outrage not just Parisian society, but even his circle of close friends. In 1890, two years after writing "Clair de lune" **(recommended 2)**, he met and fell in love with Gabrielle Dupont. Little is known about Gaby, as he called her. In fact, even back then she was considered an enigmatic figure. What appears to be true, though, is that she supported Debussy through many of these years, earning money *some*how, and allowing Debussy the freedom to compose. Indeed, some suggested she must be a woman of ill-repute, to be able to bring in money from nowhere. Debussy's friend, the playwright René Peter, wrote at the time that she *"indulged his whims and was impervious to reason . . . He emptied his purse without stopping to think where the next day's dinner would come from. And while he was lost in thought, in company with his genius, Gaby would be out raising money on knick-knacks at some sordid pawnshop"*.

The year 1893 came and Debussy, no doubt with borrowed money, went to see a play at the Bouffes-Parisiens theatre. It was *Pelléas et Mélisande* by Maeterlinck, which captivated Debussy from the start.

Fortunately, around this time, he was befriended by the composer Chausson who was much wealthier and also pretty well-connected. Through the 1880s, Chausson supported Debussy both directly and indirectly, giving him money and putting him up for work. He arranged for Debussy to play piano for himself and his circle – for which Debussy received 250 francs per month. Chausson also rented an apartment on Debussy's behalf. One night in particular, in February of 1894, a larger than normal crowd gathered to hear Debussy play the entire first act of Wagner's *Parsifal*, a performance which earned Debussy a very useful 1,000 francs.

As a result of all Chausson's help, Debussy was able to live the lifestyle of the Paris artist. He also managed to finish work on his new orchestral score: *Prélude à l'après-midi d'un faune.*
(recommended **3**)

In 1894, Debussy's love-life began to implode. Although still seeing Gaby, he met, fell in love with and – here's the amazing bit – became engaged to a woman called Thérèse Roger. It all ended in tears, though, partly due to the rumours of the nature of his liaison with Gaby, and the engagement was broken off the same year.

A year later, Debussy finished work on a new opera – *Pelléas and Mélisande.* (recommended **4**) Ever since he had seen Maeterlinck's play, he had been obsessed with setting it to music. Music, however, was now about to take a backseat in Debussy's life. In 1897, Gaby attempted to take her own life, and failed. By this time, Debussy was already seeing another woman, Lily Texier and had discarded Gaby. By 1898, the arrangement for playing the odd piece of Wagner for Chausson and his friends had fallen through and so money was a problem. Without Gaby's support, he was prosecuted for non-payment of debt. He was in dire financial straits. Within the year, he had married Lily and some sense of equilibrium was restored. He took on more piano pupils – at five francs per hour – and was able to carry on composing, producing his nocturnes in 1900.

In 1901, he was thrown an important financial lifeline. He landed a job writing music criticism for the Paris arts paper, *La revue blanche*. *Pour le piano* was written in 1902, *Estampes* in 1903 – the same year he was appointed Chevalier of the Legion of Honour. His love-life was still tempestuous, though – in fact, more tempestuous than ever. Even some of his best friends would desert him when they discovered what he did next.

In 1904, Debussy left his wife to go and live with Emma Bardac, the wife of a wealthy Paris banker, Raoul Bardac. He and Emma moved into a rented apartment, initially using her money. Any thoughts that he might have been motivated by money, though, are misplaced. Indeed, over the next ten years, despite clearly improving financial prospects, it was Debussy who struggled to keep Emma in the life to which she had become accustomed.

Amazingly, with all this going on, his composing was proceeding unchecked. That same year, 1904, he produced his gorgeous *Danse profane*. A year later – the year Emma gave birth to Debussy's daughter, who he always referred to as ChouChou – he finished his orchestral vision of the sea, *La Mer*. Indeed, it should be pointed out that he was on one of his many trips abroad at the time – to England, in fact – when he actually completed *La Mer*. At least part of it was inspired by "La Mer d'Eastbourne", where Debussy's hotel room looked out over the *"very English"* sea, as he put it.

By the time ChouChou was four, Debussy's monetary situation was beginning to look decidedly rosier. Henry Wood, founder of the Proms, offered him a fee of 100 guineas to come to London to conduct a concert – that's the equivalent of around £7,500 today. Naturally, after a little touchiness – he initially ranted that *"Caruso was being paid 400 guineas"* but calmed down when assured this was not the case – he accepted the fee. Besides, it left him time to write lovely little easy piano pieces for his daughter – a suite called *Children's Corner*. recommended **5**

In 1909, Debussy's finances appeared to continue on the right path: by now he had been given an allowance of 500 francs per month for his publishing rights; *Pelléas et Mélisande* was nearing its 80th performance; and the composer Gabriel Fauré threw him another important lifeline. He invited him to be on the governing council of the Paris Conservatoire, a job which brought with it a modest but important stipend. It made Debussy considerably more comfortable and he continued composing apace, producing his first book of preludes in 1910. (recommended **6**)

These were interesting times for Debussy. He was touring extensively as a conductor, largely to keep the money coming in; it was said that conducting was something he neither liked doing nor excelled at. *Pelléas et Mélisande* had reached its 100th performance and, when Diaghilev transformed the *Prélude à l'après-midi d'un faune* into a spectacle for the Paris-based ballet company, Ballets Russes, in 1912, Debussy was considerably cheered. A year later, however, the young upstart Stravinsky set the Ballet Russes audience rioting over his *The Rite of Spring*, and Debussy's ballet appeared eclipsed.

When 1914 arrived, Debussy spent the war years stuck in Paris – a Paris under siege from the Russians. By this time, he was living with the spectre of cancer, diagnosed some five years earlier. Incidentally, one of his last compositions, the *Berceuse héroïque*, was commissioned by our very own *Daily Telegraph*. When he died, to the sound of the bombardment of Paris on 25 March 1918, he left unfinished a potentially huge commission for an opera based on *The Fall of the House of Usher*.

That's Debussy tallied. On the whole, he was a composer who was often in severe financial problems and, even when the going was good, never really made a fortune.

RECOMMENDED LISTENING

"EN BATEAU" FROM *PETITE SUITE*
Patrick Gallois/South West German Chamber
Orchestra/Emmanuel Krivine

"CLAIR DE LUNE" FROM *SUITE BERGAMASQUE*
Zoltán Kocsis

PRÉLUDE À L'APRÈS-MIDI D'UN FAUNE
Cleveland Orchestra/Pierre Boulez

CONCERT SUITE FROM *PELLÉAS AND MÉLISANDE*
Berlin Philharmonic Orchestra/Claudio Abbado

CHILDREN'S CORNER
Jean-Yves Thibaudet

"LA CATHEDRAL ENGLOUTIE" FROM *PRELUDES BOOK 1*
Pascal Rogé

BACH'S NOTES

Name:	Johann Sebastian Bach
Nationality:	German
Born:	23 March 1685

That's the same year as ... The Monmouth Rebellion

Died:	28 July 1750

The same year as ... Gray's Elegy Written in a Country Churchyard

Wealth rating:	🏛🏛🏛

Johann Sebastian Bach was born in the German town of Eisenach on 23 March 1685, into a family business, the business being music. The young composer's father died when he was ten, leaving Johann Sebastian and his brother, Johann Jacob, in the hands of his *"rather impecunious stepmother"*, as some sources describe her. At an early age, money would have been something of an issue for J.S. He and his brother went off to live with their elder brother, Johann Christoph, who was already a successful 24-year-old organist. The move was to prove very useful for Bach in that he was given free organ lessons from his brother who, in his time, had taken organ lessons from Johann Pachelbel (of Canon in D fame). Money was obviously tight, though, and J.S. applied for and won a charitable scholarship to the Michaelischule in Lüneberg, where he went from the age of 15.

After three years in school – three years in which he immersed himself in virtually every form of music he could get his hands on – he gained his first paid job. On 9 August 1703, Bach was appointed as organist at the Neukirche in Arnstadt, a post for which he was paid the sum of around 80 thalers – not a large salary for the time, but fine as a first job, and certainly enough to support a single man of 18. One thing it probably didn't cover, though, was an extended stay in Lübeck. Bach is said to have walked there to hear and meet one of the most famous composers and organists of the day, Dietrich Buxtehude. How he raised the money to pay for this now legendary trip is still a mystery.

Bach's time in Arnstadt was not the happiest of his life. He was constantly in dispute with his bosses, not least because of the long break to see Buxtehude. After four years there, though, things took a turn for the better. He was given a new, better job – and with it a rise.

Bach hit Mülhausen in 1607, just in time to see a large part of the city burn down. By now, he was on an increased salary of 85 thaler. Feeling more comfortable, perhaps, not just with his increased wealth but with his more senior position which commanded a lot more respect, he decided to marry. He and his second cousin, Anna Barbara, were wed the same year. But he was soon to be on the move again. By 1708, he had been spotted by a duke – Duke Wilhelm Ernst of Saxe-Weimar, to be precise – and Bach was offered the job of organist and chamber musician in Weimar. With the job came a salary of 130 thaler and 6 groschen, as well as the *"right to bounties in kind"*. He had also developed a little extra sideline – organ testing. He was paid to play and approve new or repaired organs, something which attests to his growing reputation. It was one such job, testing the organ at Arnstadt, which had led directly to him getting his first job. The importance of this moonlighting really can't be over-estimated. When he tested the rebuilt organ in Leipzig's Paulinerkirche in December 1717, he was paid a fee of 20 thalers – enough money to purchase a whole houseful of furniture.

The Toccata and Fugue in D minor for organ is, arguably, Bach's most famous piece. So, if we were to price it up and work out how much Bach earned from this one work alone, what would the answer be? Well, in actual fact the answer is probably nothing – on account of the fact that he almost certainly didn't even write it. Sorry if this comes as a shock but the Toccata and Fugue is now almost always listed in the academic catalogues as, at best, *"spurious and doubtful"* and, at worst, from the pen of another. (The mighty *Grove Dictionary of Music and Musicians*, for example, lists it as such.) And if that's not bad enough, there are those who maintain that it wasn't even written for organ, but for solo violin. So, when you next hear this Vincent Price-like music, start an argument by telling everyone it's not by Bach at all, and possibly not even for organ. ⬤recommended **1**⬤

When Bach was 32 years old he was spotted by Prince Leopold of Anhalt-Cöthen. The prince offered Bach a job and Bach accepted. The only problem was that Bach already had a job – with Duke Wilhelm Ernst. Wilhelm Ernst didn't want to lose Bach, either. It must have been very nice to be popular, but not so nice when Wilhelm Ernst actually placed Bach under house arrest to stop him leaving. Yes, it did happen – Bach was placed under house arrest in order to prevent him leaving and taking up a new post. Eventually, though, he was released and, as far as he is concerned, all his Christmases appeared to come at once. Prince Leopold was very wealthy indeed and paid Bach an incredible 400 thaler, as well as generously backdating his money to cover the time spent under house arrest. Bach was no doubt a very happy man at this point.

One of the odd things about Bach's happy time at Cöthen was that it didn't stop him putting feelers out for more work elsewhere. One such occasion arose in 1719, after he'd been at Cöthen for just a couple of years. He went to pick up a new harpsichord in Berlin and, while he was there, played for a local big cheese, Christian Ludwig. It wasn't until two years later – by which time Bach's wife had died – that he decided to write to Christian Ludwig enclosing a set of six concertos. Strictly speaking, these six concertos would have been sent as a gift, but with a heavy subtext which said: *"Hey, look what I can do – and if you'd like to pay me for these there is a lot more where they came from."* There would also have been a hope that Christian Ludwig might give Bach a post. As far as history can tell, though, the six concertos elicited no response whatsoever and, as a result, almost certainly earned Bach no money whatsoever. Now they go by the name of the title used by Christian Ludwig, who was the Margrave of Brandenburg: the *Brandenburg Concertos*. **recommended 5**

Back in Cöthen, Bach was still sitting pretty. Nevertheless, he was restless. Just one year before the *Brandenburgs*, while Bach was away accompanying the prince at his spa in Carlsbad, his wife, Maria Barbara, had died. He married again the next year to Anna Magdalena Wilcken, a singer. This proved to be a very useful marriage.

Bach's nuptials were to prove very important to his financial position. In fact, let's just take a snapshot of Bach in Cöthen in 1721. He had had seven children by his first wife, four of whom were still alive. He would have another 13 children by his second wife – 20 in all, nine of whom survived to adulthood. Bach was on 400 thalers per year. But take into account that one ream of 480 bi-folios of manuscript paper cost two gulden and six groschen, and that the three things Bach loved most – tobacco, coffee and alcohol – were disproportionately expensive then compared to now, and you soon begin to see how having another court singer on a salary in the family might make a great deal of sense.

Bach did, of course, have his moonlighting job, testing organs. He could always sell manuscripts of his works, too. Ironically, although nowadays original manuscripts far outweigh printed music in price, back then, it was the opposite way round – printed music was valued much more highly over manuscript copies. Nevertheless, Bach could still sell, say, his *Keyboard Works Book 2*, for 18 groschen, and his *Keyboard Works Book 3* for three thaler (perhaps the latter's higher price reflected Bach's increased reputation by the time of the third book).

Bach was now 38 and he had itchy feet again, partly due to the fact that Prince Leopold had taken a wife who was not the slightest bit interested in music and the arts. In 1722, Bach applied for the post of Kantor in Leipzig's Thomaskirche. A year later, he eventually got the job – but only after two others had turned it down (one of them being Georg Philip Telemann).

Unfortunately, Bach was now back to being a public servant, paid both by the church and the Leipzig town council. It was quite a job, too – writing music for four churches, as well as teaching and running the Collegium Musicum – a body of musicians. As a result, no real single record exists of how much Bach was actually earning. One thing we do know is that he was paid extra for what were called *"accidentien"* – occasional payments for such things as weddings and funerals. But, as Bach himself complained in his letters, these were open to cancellation and couldn't always be relied upon. Nevertheless, by 1727 he'd managed to complete three entire annual cycles of cantatas as well as the *St John Passion*, the *St Matthew Passion* and *Magnificat*.

recommended **7**

Leipzig was certainly the most varied and prolific period of Bach's life and this – combined with the fact that he had left a job paying 400 thaler – leads to the conclusion that it was probably his most lucrative. As well as the church music, he played for one-offs too: the birthday concert for August the Strong in May 1727, for example, and the audience with Emperor Frederick the Great himself in 1742, which resulted in Bach's *A Musical Offering*. As the story goes, *A Musical Offering* is the published version of a set of pieces Bach improvised to a tune of the emperor's, given to him on the spot.

By now, of course, Bach had become *"old Bach"*. His son, C.P.E. Bach, was the court harpsichordist to the emperor, and so, when the by-then 57-year-old Johann Sebastian was drafted in to help out with the music, it must have been with a mixture of respect as well as sympathy. Bach's health was also deteriorating and this must have cost him quite dearly in medical bills. He would eventually be treated for cataracts by the same doctor who had treated Handel, John Taylor – unsuccessfully in both cases, it should be added. As a result, it is almost certain that Bach himself wouldn't have been able to play his own piece, the *Goldberg Variations.* These variations were allegedly written at the request of Johann Gottlieb Goldberg, who needed gentle music to help his patron, the Russian ambassador, Count Keyserlingk, to sleep at night. recommended **8**

From this point on, Bach grew weaker and weaker. As well as the cataracts, he almost certainly suffered from diabetes mellitus, and he eventually died on 28 July 1750.

So, the final tally. Well, as we've seen, Bach was almost continuously *"modestly prosperous"* throughout the whole of his life, and almost certainly got a raise in each successive job. Although he died without having made a will, a quick look at a list of his possessions on death reveals someone who was pretty comfortable. He owned a number of expensive musical instruments – three claviers with pedal boards, a valuable veneered harpsichord, two lute harpsichords, a violin and a lute. The lute alone was valued at 21 thalers. There were also 80 volumes of books, coins and medallions, which he'd no doubt received as presents, as well as a number of his manuscripts. All in all, he was a pretty solvent composer.

RECOMMENDED LISTENING

 TOCCATA AND FUGUE IN D MINOR
Ton Koopman

 FUGUE IN G, "THE JIG", BWV 577
Ton Koopman

 ORCHESTRAL SUITE NO. 3 IN D *(includes the "Air on the G string")*
City of London Sinfonia/Andrew Watkinson

PRELUDE NO. 1 FROM *24 PRELUDES AND FUGUES* (*the composer Charles Gounod, added a new tune over the top of Bach's Prelude to make his* Ave Maria)
Angela Hewitt

 CONCERTO NO. 5 FROM *THE BRANDENBURG CONCERTOS*
Academy of St Martin-in-the-Fields/Murray Perahia

 PARTITA NO. 3 FOR SOLO VIOLIN
Hilary Hahn

 MAGNIFICAT
The Sixteen/The Sixteen Orchestra/Harry Christophers

 "ARIA" FROM THE *GOLDBERG VARIATIONS*
YoYo Ma/Amsterdam Baroque Orchestra/Ton Koopman

 "CUM SANCTO SPIRITU" FROM THE *B MINOR MASS*
Leipzig Radio Chorus/Dresden State Orchestra/ Peter Schreier

ROSSINI'S NOTES

Name:	Gioacchino Rossini
Nationality:	Italian
Born:	29 February 1792

That's the same year that ... Shelley was born

Died:	13 November 1868

The same year that ... Renoir painted The Skaters

Wealth rating:	£££££

Gioacchino Rossini was born on 29 February 1792 in the small Adriatic coastal town of Pesaro in Italy. His father was a rather ne'er-do-well town trumpeter and his mother a locally-famous jobbing opera singer. The family was by no means wealthy but, mainly through his mother's musical earnings, Rossini was lucky enough to have been tutored in piano, viola and horn by the time he reached his early teens. Being very much a mother's boy, he would accompany his mother to many of her singing jobs, a pastime that would give him a deep-seated love of opera for the rest of his life. He was also very much in demand as a gifted boy soprano and, even in later years when his voice had changed, possessed an impressive vocal technique.

When the family upped and moved to Bologna, Rossini attended the Liceo Musicale: by the time he left, he had a bulging portfolio of compositions under his belt – quite an achievement when you consider that he paid much of his own way through college by taking on work singing in concerts in the evenings.

He wrote his first opera at the age of 16 – for no money or commission in itself. It did, however, lead directly to his first paid commission for an opera called *The Bill of Marriage*. Despite the commission, he still probably earned precious little from it.

However, it was to be the first of many: Rossini now had a foot in the opera-house door.

More opera commissions followed, none paying an absolute fortune, but some offering what Rossini called *"a satisfactory initial payment"* as well as exemption from military service. In 1812, military exemption was probably pretty useful. His opera *Tancredi* was the work that transferred him from small to big time. It was commissioned by *La Fenice* opera house in Venice, from where it transferred after a triumphant run to virtually every opera house in Europe. Rossini was well on the way to superstardom.

"The Rice Aria" from *Tancredi* went on to be one of the biggest hit-songs of its era – as big, if not bigger than "La donna è mobile" was to prove for Verdi, some years later.

Tancredi catapulted Rossini's name all over Europe. When he had another hit with his next opera, *The Italian Girl in Algiers*, he was immediately signed up by one of the big names in Italian opera promotion at the time, Domenico Barbaia. His contract was for 8,000

COMPOSERS' NOTES NOTE

Basmati pants

One of Rossini's "claims to fame", as it were, was his ability to write not only *lots* of music but lots of music quickly. Often, he would write overtures or arias just the night before the opening of an opera. His aria "Di tanti palpiti" from *Tancredi* is very often known as "The Rice Aria", so called because Rossini is said to have written it in four-minutes flat, while keeping an eye on rice, cooking in his kitchen. recommended *1*

to 12,000 francs per year, for which he had to write only two operas a year. Rossini eagerly signed on the dotted line and, by the age of 21, was famous throughout all Italy.

Three years later, and by now in Naples, he was commissioned to write an opera for the Teatro Argentino. Once again, he wasted no time – he was reputed to have written the opera in only 13 days: all 600 pages of it. And yet it would become his calling card for many years to come. It was *The Barber of Seville* and, despite Rossini's fame, it's interesting to note that his fee for writing the opera – several hundred pounds – was nevertheless not as much as the main singers were being paid to sing it. **recommended 2**, **recommended 3** and **recommended 4**

The name Rossini was now almost as admired across Italy as Verdi's would be 40 years later. Money-wise, in 1822, three things helped the Rossini coffers. One was his latest opera, *Semiramide*. Another was a mini-tour of Vienna. The third, though, was by far the most profitable. He married the soprano Isabella Colbran, a singer who had appeared in many of his operas. She came with a dowry of 40,000 scudi – equivalent to around £50,000 today.

A year later, in 1823, Rossini decided to "do a Haydn", as it were. That is, he was invited on a money-making tour of London. He hit town on 13 December, staying at number 90, Regent Street. While in the capital, he acted as musical director for a short season of his own operas at the King's Theatre, in Haymarket, a season in which his wife starred. She alone was earning fees varying from £1,000 to £1,500 per opera, and it's said that, overall, after his London tour, Rossini was better off to the tune of tens of thousands of pounds. Some idea of his earning potential can be gained from the lessons he gave. It seemed anyone who was anyone wanted a music lesson from the famous Rossini while he was in town. So instead of charging the going rate of one guinea per hour, Rossini charged 100 guineas, and still got more pupils than he could fit in. As a footnote to the tour, it's also said that he sang duets with George IV, and was generally hailed as not just Italy's but the world's greatest composer.

When Rossini left London, he made Paris his home, going on to write both *Le Comte Ory* and his spectacular version of *William Tell*. Just to compose *William Tell*, Rossini demanded 6,000 francs per year for life from Emperor Charles X – a figure which was duly paid. The publisher Eugene-Theodore Troupenas also paid Rossini a further 24,000 for the publishing rights. recommended **5**

Having produced yet another hit opera, this time the ever popular *William Tell*, Rossini now wanted for nothing, financially. He then made a famous decision. He put down his pen and stopped composing. More or less. He did keep his hand in a few years later, when he wrote a version of the *Stabat Mater* for a friend, the priest and statesman Fernandez Varela. (Having said that, Rossini never actually found time to finish it. It ended up having to be "ghost-composed", as it were, by one of his disciples, Giovanni Tadolini.) Rossini's fee for the *Stabat Mater* was one gold, diamond-encrusted snuff box. Well, what do you pay the man who has everything?   recommended **6**

Rossini's decision to quit composing has always begged two questions. Firstly, why stop, obviously, but secondly, just what did he do with his time?

To answer the second question first, Rossini cooked. Not all the time, of course, but his passion for food and general hospitality did become legendary. An invite to Rossini's for dinner was a much-coveted ticket where the great man himself did the cooking. He even left us with a number of his own recipes, the most famous of which is *Tournedos Rossini* – beef with foie gras and white toasted bread. He also found time to take a mistress – the quaintly named Olympe Pélissier – who became the second Mrs Rossini when the first died in 1845. Beyond that, he would entertain with his legendary soirées in which he and his friends would play, sing and, of course, eat.

The answer to the first question is not quite as easy. Some say he simply wanted to live a more enjoyable life, without the ever-present deadlines of opera composing. Some, of course, say that he ran out of ideas. One powerful theory, though, is the emergence of Meyerbeer on the Paris opera scene. For three years before *William Tell*, Meyerbeer was enjoying greater and greater success in the French capital, with grander and grander works. By 1831, two years after *William Tell*, Meyerbeer's opera *Robert le Diable* was the talk of the town. Some think that Rossini simply didn't want to compete with the new wunderkind – or risk losing the battle. Even so, rivalry between the two composers was never far from the surface, as the *Composers' Notes Note* on page 119 shows.

Rossini did, though, come out of this self-imposed retirement one last time, and that was in 1863, by which time he was 71. Despite perhaps not being the most religious of men, it was to compose a mass – the *Petite Messe Solennelle*. This was written to no particular commission but more for his own composing pleasure. In it, he can't resist having a little fun either – the musical tempo marking in one section reads "Allegro christiano" It's a lovely, occasionally over-the-top little work, and has become one of his most popular. **recommended 7**

The "little mass" was written in 1863 and Rossini died not long after, on 13 November 1868. In his will, he left a very healthy estate which, at today's values, would run into hundreds of thousands of pounds.

COMPOSERS' NOTES NOTE

Rossini qua non

Rossini is famous for his acid tongue and "bon mots", the most famous being his comment that Wagner had some wonderful moments but some awful quarters of an hour. On one occasion, he was visited by an aspiring young composer who had brought two of his piano pieces for the composer to hear. Rossini agreed to listen and say which of the two he preferred. As the young composer finished the first piece, Rossini smiled, stood up and said: *"You don't need to play any more. I prefer the second."*

RECOMMENDED LISTENING

 "DI TANTI PALPITI" FROM *TANCREDI*
Ewa Podles/Hungarian State Opera Orchestra/Pier Giorgio Morandi

 OVERTURE FROM *THE BARBER OF SEVILLE*
Philharmonia Orchestra/Carlo Maria Giulini

 "UNA VOCE POCO FA" FROM *THE BARBER OF SEVILLE*
Frederica von Stade/Rotterdam Philharmonic Orchestra/Edo de Waart

 "LARGO AL FACTOTUM" FROM *THE BARBER OF SEVILLE*
Thomas Hampson/Tuscan Orchestra/Gianluigi Gelmetti

 OVERTURE FROM *WILLIAM TELL*
Philharmonia Orchestra/Carlo Maria Giulini

 STABAT MATER
Bavarian Radio Symphony Orchestra/Chor des Bayerischen Rundfunks/Semyon Bychkov

 PETITE MESSE SOLENNELLE
The King's Consort/Robert King

BERLIOZ'S NOTES

Name:	Hector Berlioz
Nationality:	French
Born:	11 December 1803

That's the same year that ... the Caledonian Canal was built

Died:	8 March 1869

The same year that ... Frank Lloyd Wright was born

Wealth rating: 🏦🏦🏦

Hector Berlioz was born on 11 December 1803 in La Cote-Saint-Andre, a small town in the east of France, not far from Grenoble. His father was a successful and financially comfortable doctor who looked after his son's education personally, tutoring him in Latin, music and the classics. Despite the fact that his father was an ardent music lover, Berlioz was nevertheless expected to take up his father's trade and so, despite learning flute, singing and guitar, he was duly packed off to a Paris medical school at the age of 18. Not surprisingly, he abandoned medicine just a year or so into his course and enrolled himself at the Paris Conservatoire. His musicality quickly began to show through and he wrote his *Missa Solemnis* in 1824, although he didn't manage to raise the funds to have it performed until a full year later. At this stage, his father was still supporting him with an allowance, with the proviso that the money would cease if he failed at music. His mother was not quite so accommodating. She considered he was bringing shame on his family by choosing the life of an artist, and it may have been her intervention that eventually led her husband to stop his son's allowance completely in 1826.

So, at the age of 23, Berlioz was broke. To keep *some* money coming in, he gained a job as a chorus singer at a vaudeville theatre. Not particularly proud of his new-found career, he made sure he kept it secret from most of his friends.

In September 1827 Berlioz went to see a production of *Hamlet* which featured a well-known Irish actress, Harriet Smithson. It was an important meeting for Berlioz: Smithson would become one of the dominant forces in Berlioz's life – an obsession, even. Initially, Smithson thought Berlioz was mad – she was, after all, a famous actress and he was, as yet, a nobody in the world of music.

In August 1830, on his third attempt, Berlioz eventually won the prestigious French composition prize of the Prix de Rome, and set out to spend three years in the Italian capital – part of the winner's reward. By this time, his father had restored his allowance, and so things were financially a little easier. On his return to Paris, he set about recapturing the heart of Harriet Smithson by staging a concert of the work he had written just a couple of years earlier: the *Symphonie fantastique*. **recommended 1**

The plan to "say it with music" appears to have worked. Following the concert, Harriet Smithson agreed to meet him and things went well. So well, in fact, that on 3 October 1833 they were married, with the composer Franz Liszt acting as a witness. However, Smithson was probably using Berlioz as a way out of debt, as her acting career was failing rapidly.

Money-wise, though, things were about to take a turn for the better for Berlioz himself. After a concert in December 1833, he was visited backstage by the composer Niccolò Paganini, who had been in the audience. Paganini was, at this point, one of the most successful performers of his age and was on the lookout for new music to show off his phenomenal technique. He would eventually compose six violin concertos of his own, but for now, he was impressed enough with Berlioz to commission a new piece which could demonstrate his prowess on the viola. Berlioz accepted the challenge and set to work. The resulting piece, however, was not to Paganini's liking. Berlioz had made the viola part too low-profile and Paganini never played the piece.

The two composers fell out and remained out of contact for quite a few years. The work was *Harold in Italy*. **recommended 2**

In August 1834, Berlioz's wife Harriet gave birth to a son, Louis, although this did nothing to shore up an already failing marriage. With her career faded, Harriet took to drink and eventually Berlioz moved out of the family home, in the end taking a girlfriend – the opera singer, Marie Recio.

The next few years saw Berlioz producing some of his best work. It's important to remember that, in his time, Berlioz was very much the avant garde of French music, composing works which, although now considered standard pieces of the classical repertoire, were controversial and hard-going in their day. To keep enough money coming in, he took up a career as a journalist, writing for the *Journal des Débats*, a well-respected Paris publication.

On 16 December 1838, Paganini turned up, unannounced, at a performance of *Harold in Italy* and was enchanted by the piece that he had rejected some five years earlier. When the work finished, he leapt out of his seat, mounted the stage and knelt at Berlioz's feet, hailing the piece as a work of genius. The next day, he sent Berlioz a note: *"Beethoven is dead,"* it read, *"and Berlioz alone can revive him."* With it was a Rothschild banker's draft for 20,000 francs. The money funded much of his following work, including the dramatic symphony *Romeo and Juliet*. **recommended 3**

From 1840, it appears that Berlioz managed to keep the commissions rolling in, very often from the French government. With each new piece, Berlioz seemed to get more and more spectacular. The concerts he conducted were also becoming more and more extravagant: in 1844, his performance of Beethoven's fifth symphony included 36 double basses. A performance of Weber's *Der Freischütz* featured 24 french horns, and an extract of a Rossini opera used 25 harps. One concert involved 1,200 performers in one evening and laid Berlioz open to ridicule from the critics of the day.

Berlioz didn't seem to care, though. He was pushing the boundaries of his art, as he saw it, and managing to earn enough at the same time. His standing as probably the most famous French composer was not in doubt and his creativity was showing no signs of abating.

From here on in, it would appear money worries were a thing of the past for Berlioz. He made more or less successful tours of England and Russia, and witnessed a festival of his music, overseen by his champion, Liszt. One part that didn't go according to plan was a portion of the English tour. He was engaged as a conductor for a season at the Drury Lane theatre in London, doing programmes of Mozart and Donizetti. The entrepreneur Louis Jullien, however, went bankrupt, leaving Berlioz unpaid. A concert at the Hanover Square Concert Rooms proved more successful and firmly established his reputation over here.

Another hiccup proved to be a premiere in 1846. Money-wise, it wasn't a success. As Berlioz recounted in his

COMPOSERS' NOTES NOTE

Grande Messe to pay the Mort-gage

Berlioz's favourite of his own works was his requiem. *"If I were threatened with destruction of all my works but one, I would beg mercy for the* Grande messe des morts,*"* he once said. It was written for the French Ministry of the Interior, but Berlioz was eventually paid for it by the War Ministry. They initially tried to pay him with a medal instead of money. Berlioz turned down the medal, the légion d'honneur, insisting on the more traditional *"francs and centimes."*

recommended **4**

memoirs: *"The first performance was a serious reverse . . . financially. {It} was given twice before a half-empty house. The fashionable Paris audience . . . stayed comfortably at home."* This was the premiere of *The Damnation of Faust.* recommended **6**

On the whole, though, Berlioz was solvent and getting work. Yet despite this, he himself felt that he was a failure as a composer. The challenging nature of his music meant that it was not loved by the French in the way that the Italians would love the music of Verdi.

Add to this, failing health, a tempestuous second marriage, and the death of his son from yellow fever and it seemed that the fates were conspiring to make Berlioz's later years very miserable. When he died, on 8 March 1869, his coffin was carried to its final resting place by a band of famous French composers, Gounod among them.

RECOMMENDED LISTENING

 "THE MARCH TO THE SCAFFOLD" FROM *SYMPHONIE FANTASTIQUE*
Concertgebouw Orchestra Amsterdam/Mariss Jansons

 HAROLD IN ITALY
Nobuko Imai/London Symphony Orchestra/Sir Colin Davis

 "QUEEN MAB SCHERZO" FROM *ROMEO AND JULIET*
Boston Symphony Orchestra/Charles Munch

 GRANDE MESSE DES MORTS
London Symphony Orchestra and Chorus/Sir Colin Davis

 "ROMAN CARNIVAL OVERTURE" FROM *BENVENUTO CELLINI*
Boston Symphony Orchestra/Charles Munch

 "HUNGARIAN MARCH" FROM *THE DAMNATION OF FAUST*
Orchestre des Concerts Lamoureux/Igor Markevitch

VERDI'S NOTES

Name:	Giuseppe Verdi
Nationality:	Italian
Born:	9 October 1813

That's the same year that ... Jane Austen wrote Pride and Prejudice

Died:	27 January 1901

The same year that ... Picasso began his Blue period

Wealth rating:	£££££

Let's allow Verdi himself to tell us how it was in the beginning:

"Alas. Born poor," he wrote, *"in a poor village, I hadn't the means of acquiring any education; they put a wretched spinet under my hands and, some time after that, I started writing notes . . . notes one after the other . . . And the fact is that, now I'm an old man, I have great doubts as to the value of those notes."*

That's Verdi's brief account of his early life.

The poor village he spoke of was Le Roncole, near Bussetto in the province of Parma. Verdi was born there on 9 October 1813. His father was a local innkeeper and, when his son was only eight, he did indeed raise enough cash to buy a second-hand spinet. It was obviously something Verdi took to very quickly because, by the age of only ten, he was appointed organist at a church in Le Roncole. He was lodging in Bussetto at the time, so that he could attend school, and therefore had to walk the six-mile round trip to Le Roncole every Sunday, for which he was paid a princely sum equivalent to £4.

In June 1832, when Verdi's father was turned down for a grant to send his son to the Milan Conservatory, a local benefactor named Barezzi stepped in and agreed to fund the four-year course. Verdi was duly packed off to sit the entrance exam, which, amazingly, he failed. So, Barezzi paid for lodgings and a private composition teacher in Milan. Verdi became a member of the local *filodrammatici* or Philharmonic Society, where he began to get noticed for his ability to play and conduct. He was appointed as Bussetto's music director in 1836, the same year that he married his benefactor's daughter, Margherita. He spent three years running the small town's music, all the while keeping an eye firmly on the bright lights of the bigger cities. As soon as his three-year contract was up, Verdi moved to Milan.

Financially, at first, Verdi lived off cash gifts from his father-in-law. Musically, though, he had spent his time in Bussetto wisely and had arrived in Milan complete with a finished opera – *Oberto, conte di San Bonifacio*. It received its first performance on 17 November 1839 at the famous La Scala opera house. Verdi's composing career was underway and, more importantly, he had been spotted. The publisher Ricordi bought the rights to his score for 2,000 Austrian lire and offered him a contract with La Scala for three more operas, to be given at eight-month intervals.

In the period leading up to his next opera, however, money became tight, and his wife Margherita was forced to pawn jewellery. In the same year – 1840 – disaster struck. Margherita died, leaving Verdi distraught. However, he honoured his contract for the new opera, *Un giorno di regno*. It was a flop. Verdi was down and nearly out. The Milan impresario, Merelli, though, persuaded him to accept a new libretto on the story of Nebuchadnezzar, and this was to prove a turning point. Its premiere and instant success on 9 March 1842 made him an overnight sensation. Society at once opened its doors to him. He met Donizetti. He met Rossini. *"With* Nabucco*,"* he wrote, *"my career can be said to have begun."*

recommended *1*

With Nabucco, Verdi had both turned around a tragic part of his life and made himself a hot musical property. The commissioning committee at La Fenice, the opera house in

Venice, quickly commissioned his next opera, for which Verdi requested a fee of 12,000 Austrian lire. He had heard that Bellini had been paid 10,000 for *Norma* and he decided that his stock was high enough to gain more. The fee was agreed and Verdi set to work on *I Lombardi*. He followed it with *Ernani*, the story of a revolutionary, which was a huge success despite a poor production. *Ernani* achieved what even *Nabucco* had not – it made Verdi famous outside Italy as well as within.

The next few years of Verdi's life saw him go from strength to strength. Personally, he renewed his friendship with one of the sopranos who had sung in his previous operas, Giuseppina Strepponi, and, after living together for several years, they were married in 1859.

Verdi toured Europe, supervising the staging of his early operas, including a successful run of *I due foscari* in London. During this time, he made his money mainly through performance and publishing rights. Verdi, it appears, was quite a businessman, having also purchased property following the success of *Ernani*. He sold at a profit, allowing him to buy his parents family home, the Fattoria Sant'Agata, some two miles outside Bussetto, as well as the Palazzo Dordoni in Busetto itself. Indeed, by 1850, he had made enough money to retire.

Of course, Verdi didn't want to retire. One year later, he produced his biggest hit to date. It's said that, soon after its premiere in 1851, every barrel organ in Europe was playing the biggest hit tune of the day – "La donna è mobile". *Rigoletto* was the smash-hit opera of 1851. **recommended 2**

It is said that Verdi *knew* what a hit tune he had in "La donna è mobile" – so much so that he kept it under wraps, even from the orchestra, until the final dress rehearsal, for fear that someone would steal it.

By 1853 – two years after its successful premiere – *Rigoletto* had played in Paris, where even Victor Hugo, on whose original story the opera was based, declared it a masterpiece. Rome wanted Verdi's next opera, which it simply presumed would be a success. La Fenice was anxious to stage the one after that. For Rome, Verdi proposed an opera based on the story *El Trovador* by García Gutiérrez. For Venice, he suggested an opera based on the play he had seen at the Vaudeville Theatre in Paris, by Alexandre Dumas, called *La dame aux camélias*.

Both works were huge successes. *El Trovador* became *Il trovatore* **recommended 3** and *La dame aux camélias* was transformed into *La traviata – The Fallen Woman*. **recommended 4** and **recommended 5** (Ironically, although the more popular of the two today, *La traviata* had an awkward birth before becoming standard repertoire.) At the age of only 40, Verdi was proclaimed the greatest opera composer of his day.

Over the next seven years, Verdi almost didn't seem to be able to put a foot wrong. His next opera was for Paris and, even though he chose as his subject the massacre of the French army in Sicily, it went down a storm. It was called *Les vêpres siciliennes. Simon Boccanegra*, his subsequent project, was a rare flop at first, and only enjoyed success after Verdi revised it many years later. *Un ballo in maschera* reverted back to his winning form, and coincided with Verdi's name being daubed on the street walls across Italy – although not solely because of his music.

Verdi was a fervent supporter of the *risorgimento* in Italy – the push to reunite all the separate Italian states into one country. Verdi's credentials – i.e. nationalistic opera subjects, as well as his constant battling with the state censors – made him a popular figure in Italy, and his name was soon being put to a different use. In the phrase Viva Verdi, the letters V E R D I stood for **V**ictor **E**mmanuel **R**e **D**'Italia – Victor Emmanuel King of Italy. The connection and the publicity can have done Verdi's box office no harm at all.

In 1862, an opera commission came from an unlikely source – the Imperial Opera in St Petersburg. When the new work was premiered, following a false start and some not entirely enthusiastic reviews – this was an Italian in an increasingly nationalistic Russia, remember – Verdi nevertheless managed to turn the situation around. As well as a healthy commission fee of around 11,000 roubles, he added the Order of the Royal and Imperial Order of St Stanislaus to his list of honours. The work for St Petersburg was *La forza del destino*.   **recommended 6**

Between 1862 and 1870, Verdi continued apace. He and Giuseppina would summer in their farmhouse in Bussetto, where they were said to enjoy an almost peasant existence despite their wealth. In winter, they would stay in their palatial house in Genoa.

Although his next opera, *Don Carlos*, suffered the same fate as *Simon Boccanegra* – with endless changes being made to achieve his usual success – Verdi soon returned to winning form. His next commission was testament to his global popularity. He was commissioned by the Khedive of Egypt – Khedive loosely translates as "viceroy" – to write a new opera for the newly-built Cairo Opera House. Verdi, who insisted on being present at the premieres of his works, is thought not to have fancied the journey and the travel arrangements. As a result, he put in an astronomical request for the fee – $20,000, an enormous amount in those days. Unfortunately for him but fortunately for us, the fee was agreed and the opera written. Ironically, Verdi didn't attend the premiere in the end, which was given on Christmas Eve 1871. The khedive's assistant sent him a message to say: *"We have a success beyond belief."* The opera was *Aïda*.   **recommended 7**

That was in 1870. Verdi was 57. During the next few years, until his death in 1901 at the grand old age of 88, its fair to say that his style gradually changed – matured if you like. If you were to put his opera based on Shakespeare's *Othello* alongside something like *Rigoletto*, or *La traviata*, then you would hear a striking difference. *Otello* is a much more studied work: there is not as much of the traditional form of his earlier works or of the stand-and-deliver approach. It is, though, considered to be one of his finest works and, composed at the age of 74, it's fair enough to call it an Indian Summer piece. At 79, he then produced another opera, the great *Falstaff*, which sets a combination of the stories of Shakespeare's *The Merry Wives of Windsor* and *Henry IV*. It shows Verdi at a new, different type of creative peak. After the premiere, the King of Italy offered to make Verdi the Marchese de Bussetto. Verdi refused, however, with the line *"Io son un paesano"* – I am a peasant!

When Verdi died in 1901, he was rich beyond belief. Towards the end, he gave 2.5 million lire to found a home for aged musicians, which is still going strong today, supported by royalties from his estate. It's said that a quarter of a million people followed the funeral cortege to its final resting place.

And that's Verdi tallied. He was a very rich composer with a fine business head on his shoulders. Yet he would still have us all believe that he was a peasant at heart.

RECOMMENDED LISTENING

"VA PENSIERO" (CHORUS OF THE HEBREW SLAVES) FROM *NABUCCO*
Ambrosian Opera Chorus/Philharmonia Orchestra/Riccardo Muti

"LA DONNA È MOBILE" FROM *RIGOLETTO*
Roberto Alagna/London Philharmonic Orchestra

"ANVIL CHORUS" FROM *IL TROVATORE*
London Voices/London Symphony Orchestra/ Antonio Pappano

PRELUDE TO ACT 1 OF *LA TRAVIATA*
Orchestra of the Royal Opera House, Covent
Garden/Sir Georg Solti

 "LIBIAMO" (DRINKING SONG) FROM *LA TRAVIATA*
Luciano Pavarotti/Cheryl Studer/James Levine/
Metropolitan Opera Orchestra and Chorus

 OVERTURE FROM *LA FORZA DEL DESTINO*
New Philharmonia Orchestra/Riccardo Muti

 "CELESTE AÏDA" FROM *AÏDA*
José Cura/Philharmonia Orchestra

 "DIES IRAE" AND "TUBA MIRUM" FROM *REQUIEM*
Monteverdi Choir/Orchestre Revolutionaire et
Romantique/Sir John Eliot Gardiner

TCHAIKOVSKY'S NOTES

Name:	Peter Ilyich Tchaikovsky
Nationality:	Russian
Born:	7 May 1840

That's the same year that ... Kew Gardens opened

Died:	6 November 1893

The same year that ... Henry Ford built his first car

Wealth rating: £££

Peter Ilyich Tchaikovsky was born on 7 May 1840 in the Russian town of Kamsko-Votkinsk, about 2,000 km east of Moscow. His father was a successful mining engineer and his mother a linguist. Peter was the second of six children and he quickly became attuned to his mother's sensitive and very musical nature. She taught him piano from the age of four, but by the time he was six years old he was already being sent for more formal music lessons. Money, in these early years, was in good enough supply and the Tchaikovskys led a relatively stable existence until Peter was eight. At this point, his father resigned from his safe government job in Votinsk in the hope of a better paid post in Moscow. When this came to nothing, the entire Tchaikovsky family were thrown into a more turbulent monetary period. Nevertheless, both Peter and his brother were sent off to boarding school. It wasn't until Tchaikovsky was 12 that the family was more financially settled. They moved to St Petersburg but the stability was short lived. Two years later, Tchaikovsky's mother, his nurturing musical influence and the woman on whom he doted, died of cholera. It is often said that this was something the sensitive composer never truly got over.

By this time, aged 14, Tchaikovksy had been transferred to the St Petersburg School of Jurisprudence and so it was that, at the age of 19, he became a clerk in the Ministry of Justice. It was a secure, if modest, salary but he still managed to keep up his music lessons, with a conservative teacher named Zaremba. Tchaikovsky was 22 when he learned that Anton Rubinstein was to set up a new music conservatory in Moscow, and he immediately resigned his post at the Ministry of Justice in favour of the conservatory. It was a gamble – giving up a safe salary in the hope that his musical abilities would pay off – but it worked. Within a couple of years, Tchaikovsky was teaching harmony at the Moscow Conservatory, having been invited there by Nicholas, Anton Rubinstein's brother.

In Moscow, he lodged with Nicholas Rubinstein and immediately launched himself into his first big work, his first symphony, *Winter Dreams.* By now Tchaikovsky was 26 and the scale of the work took its toll on him. He suffered nervous disorders: hypochondria, numbness of the hands and feet, even hallucinations. The symphony was poorly received, but Tchaikovsky always retained a soft spot for it – the *"sin of my sweet youth,"* as he called it.

Nevertheless, in general, his work *was* attracting attention. He was invited to meet the group of composers who went by the name of The Five or The Mighty Handful – César Cui, Mily Balakirev, Modest Mussorgsky, Nikolai Rimsky-Korsakov and Alexander Borodin – five men who had dedicated themselves to giving Russia its nationalist voice in classical music. Tchaikovsky himself, though, was never fully committed to the cause – The Five never became *The Six*, as it were. He was more concerned with finding his *own* voice than that of Mother Russia. If the two coincided, then all well and good, but if not, so be it. He was, though, perfectly prepared to take constructive advice and help, so when, in 1869, Balakirev suggested the idea of a composition based on a Shakepeare play, Tchaikovsky set to work. With Balakirev supervising at regular intervals, the ultimate success of the piece was down to a combination of Tchaikovsky's state of mind and Balakirev's help – Tchaikovsky had recently finished a doomed love affair with a well-known singer, Désirée Artot, and so this particular Shakespeare play suited his temperament perfectly: it was *Romeo and Juliet.* **recommended 1**

After 1869, when Tchaikovsky turned 29, he was able to spend his winters in Moscow and his summers at the country estates of various friends, usually composing in these idyllic, sunshine months. The pieces that came from these stays are now pretty much forgotten, though – works like his opera, *Vakula the Smith* and the first two string quartets. *Vakula the Smith* was important to Tchaikovsky's finances, though, as it won him 1,500 roubles as first prize in a Russian Musical Society competition. That's the equivalent of around £10,000 today.

It wasn't until 1874 that he produced the next work that would stay for ever in the repertoire. It was his piano concerto, a piece he had written for Nicholas Rubinstein, but over which the two famously fell out. Rubinstein called the piece unplayable. Composer and performer did eventually make up though and, indeed, Rubinstein went on to champion the work in concert. **recommended 2**

Tchaikovsky's next major work didn't fare much better. *"I have taken on this work partly because of money and partly because I have wanted to try my hand at this sort of music for a long time."* The "sort of music" was ballet and the subject was to be *Swan Lake,* a commission from the Bolshoi Ballet Company. The year 1875 had seen the premiere of Tchaikovsky's third symphony come and go, and he was paid 300 roubles – around £2,000 – for the first performance. The first night of *Swan Lake* was a benefit performance for a retiring ballerina, and it proved to be a fiasco – poor choreography, poor sets and, in the end, a poor reaction. In addition, he received only 800 roubles – roughly £5,000 today – for the score. Sadly for Tchaikovsky, the work was given up for dead – even he himself was moved by its bad reception to condemn it. It was not performed again until two years after his death. recommended **3**

By the time *Swan Lake* had been premiered in 1877, Tchaikovsky had made the acquaintance of two women who were to have totally different effects on his life. One was Antonina Milyukova, a neurotic nymphomaniac with a penchant for tantrums and emotional blackmail. If you have ever seen the film of Tchaikovsky's life made by Ken Russell, she is the one played by Glenda Jackson. Tchaikovsky married this 28-year-old music student, but within days was unable to continue the relationship. *"Physically, she is totally repulsive to me,"* he wrote at the time, and quickly fled the marriage in favour of his sister's estate in Kamenka. He even tried to take his own life by drowning himself.

Fortunately, not long after, he met a second woman, one who was to have not only an emotionally steadying influence in his life, but also a financially crucial one, too. Nadezhda von Meck was a wealthy widow, the mother of 11 children, who initially came to Tchaikovsky with a small and unimportant music commission – but in doing so, she started one of the most important musical relationships in the history of the great composers. They eventually embarked on an arrangement whereby von Meck would give Tchaikovsky an annual allowance of 6,000 roubles – which would be worth the equivalent of around £40,000 today – but agreed that the two should never deliberately meet. As a result, Tchaikovsky not only got the financial security he needed, he also got his ideal relationship with a woman – affectionate, but only in correspondence, and sexually unthreatening. When people questioned their relationship, Tchaikovsky simply said: *"She is kind, delicate, generous and infinitely tolerant. To me, she is simply the eternally kind hand of Providence."* One of the first fruits of the new relationship, so to speak, was Tchaikovsky's fourth symphony. recommended **4**

Initially, the new-found financial security from 1881 onwards appeared to be moving Tchaikovsky to great things – the violin concerto, the *Capriccio Italien* and the *Serenade for Strings* all come from this period. But as much as his money brought him safety and security, it also brought a certain fame and recognition. Worse still, it eventually seemed to signal the start of a creative lull. Across the 1880s – up until 1888, in fact – Tchaikovsky produced little of note apart from the "Manfred" Symphony. His day settled into a routine. He would rise at seven, take tea, read the Bible, and then start work at 9.30am, sharp. As he once said: *"The Muse . . . has learned to be punctual."* In the afternoon, he walked, but always with a music notebook to hand, and then in the evening he composed again or proof-read his work.

But then in 1888, he hit a creative seam which he was able to mine until his death just five years later. It was a period of touring for Tchaikovsky – he had already toured America once before but, from this point on, he took up a punishing schedule of concerts. Nevertheless, from this period comes *Hamlet, The Sleeping Beauty* and the opera *The Queen of Spades.*

Two events that more or less coincided were the writing of the fifth symphony and Tchaikovsky's loss of Nadezhda von Meck – loss, that is, in that she terminated their financial agreement, worth, by then, 18,000 roubles a year. For Tchaikovsky, though, the cut went much deeper than mere money. By now, he was able to support himself, more or less, via appearances and commissions. The loss of his pen-friend, confidante and, arguably, maternal substitute hit him hard. The reason Von Meck gave for the ending of the allowance was her own financial hardship. When Tchaikovsky later learnt that her money troubles were at an end, he was all the more upset that the relationship was not resumed. But the fifth symphony is remarkable in the midst of all this – an exuberant, tune-filled work which is still one of his most popular today. **recommended 5**

Tchaikovsky continued his fruitful creative period into the 1890s with the music for the ballet *The Nutcracker* recommended **6**, written just one year after his split from his patron – a year that was mostly taken up with a financially rewarding, if personally exhausting, tour of the United States.

Then, in 1893, he took up work on his sixth symphony, the "Pathétique". recommended **7** He wrote at a furious pace, frequently weeping as the themes came to him, and it was all he could do to write them down. In June of that year, he travelled to Cambridge where he was given an honorary doctorate. He then returned to St Petersburg and gave the premiere of his new symphony to a bemused audience. Then, on 2 November, after a light lunch, he helped himself to a glass of tap water, much to the shock of his brother. This was November, after all, the "cholera season" in St Petersburg, and tap water was well known to be unsafe. *"But one can't go tiptoeing about in fear of death for ever!"* he reputedly said. At three o'clock in the morning, just four days later, he died. His funeral took place at the Kazan Cathedral in St Petersburg, and he is buried in the city's Alexander Nevsky cemetery.

RECOMMENDED LISTENING

FANTASY OVERTURE FROM *ROMEO AND JULIET*
Bournemouth Symphony Orchestra/Andrew Litton

PIANO CONCERTO
Martha Argerich/Berlin Philharmonic Orchestra/ Claudio Abbado

ACT II OF *SWAN LAKE*
Russian State Symphony Orchestra/Dmitri Yablonsky

recommended **4**
SYMPHONY NO. 4
London Philharmonic Orchestra/Paavo Berglund

recommended **5**
SYMPHONY NO. 5
Oslo Philharmonic Orchestra/Mariss Jansons

recommended **6**
MINIATURE OVERTURE FROM *THE NUTCRACKER*
Kirov Orchestra/Valery Gergiev

recommended **7**
"PATHÉTIQUE" SYMPHONY
Gothenburg Symphony Orchestra/Neeme Järvi

BIZET'S NOTES

Name: Georges Alexandre-César-Léopold Bizet

Nationality: French

Born: 25 October 1838
That's the same year that ... Dickens wrote Oliver Twist

Died: 3 June 1875
The same year that ... Captain Webb swam the channel

Wealth rating: 💷💷

Georges Alexandre-César-Léopold Bizet was born on 25 October 1838 in Paris. His mother and father were both very musical and his uncle was a fashionable singing teacher of the day. He was admitted to the Paris Conservatoire at the early age of 11 and he soon began winning prizes. Very soon, partly by chance, he came under the influence of Charles Gounod. Gounod's father-in-law was the counterpoint teacher at the conservatoire and, now and again, Gounod would stand in for the ageing professor. It was an influence which many believe stayed with Bizet until he died.

Bizet shone in his piano classes, eventually attracting praise from the composer Franz Liszt, but it was to composition that he was truly devoted. He was composing songs and pieces all the way through conservatoire and, by the age of 17, he had written the Symphony in C. **recommended 1** Amazingly, although it is now one of his best-known pieces, it was only discovered and performed for the first time in 1935.

Bizet was still just 17 when he entered one of his pieces in the famous French composition prize, the Prix de Rome. Oddly enough, despite his work being judged the best, he was awarded second prize. Some think his age alone prevented the judges from feeling they could award him first position. By way of consolation, he was awarded free tickets to all the theatres of

Paris, which would no doubt have proved useful to a fledgling opera composer. At the age of 19, he eventually won the Prix de Rome for his cantata *Clovis et Clotilde*, although he had to be content with sharing first place. Nevertheless, the three years studying in Italy – the main part of the prize – suited Bizet immensely and, under the Italian sun, he began to wrestle with finding his compositional voice.

Back in France three years later, he tried to assert himself on the Paris music scene, accepting a small commission to write a one-act opera. Half way through rehearsals, though, he discovered that there was a prize being offered for the best unpublished opera by any Prix de Rome prize-winner. As it turned out, the Théâtre Lyrique had been given 100,000 francs by the minister for the arts, to use specifically for new operas. Bizet immediately stopped the rehearsals of his first opera – and its planned performance – and began to write a new work. It is thought that he used much of the half-rehearsed work as the basis for his new, potential prize-winner. It was given its first performance on 30 September 1863 when Bizet would have been just 24 years old. It was a modest success back then and even today it is not very often performed. Yet it has yielded one particular superb duet which will never be forgotten. This is "Au fond du temple saint", and the opera is *The Pearl Fishers*. **recommended 2**

Around this time, Bizet spent lots of time at a country cottage built by his father in a place called Le Vésinet, which would have been, in those days, a few miles outside Paris, on the banks of the Seine. Most of his time was taken up with doing edits and rewrites for publishers, or giving piano lessons – something which he loathed doing. It was not particularly interesting work for a great composer, but at least it was financially rewarding and – along with money from accompanying other musicians – allowed him freedom to compose. In July 1866, the Théâtre Lyrique commissioned another opera. Bizet based it on Walter Scott's *The Fair Maid of Perth* and it was premiered on the 26

December 1867. This was much more favourably received than *The Pearl Fishers*, not only by the public, but also by the French press of the day.

Despite the good reception afforded *La jolie fille de Perth*, by the time Bizet hit 30, he still felt he had produced nothing which fulfilled his early promise. Just one year later, though, he married – an act which brought with it a considerable change in his financial position.

His wife, Geneviève Halévy, was the daughter of his former composition tutor at the conservatoire. She brought with her a dowry of *"between 150,000 and 200,000 francs, with 500,000 to come later"*.

Bizet moved in with Geneviève and some of her relations. One of them, Ludovic Halévy, was a librettist who had had considerable success with his work for composers such as Jacques Offenbach. This family arrangement was to prove important for Bizet, as we'll see later. For now, though, he began work on three separate librettos, passed to him by the Paris Opéra-Comique but, as with much of Bizet's work, they all came to nothing. He was working on them, in fact, when he learned of the outbreak of war between France and Prussia on 15 July 1870. Bizet immediately enlisted in the French National Guard and spent the war months – and the time of the Commune – resolutely in Paris. This badly affected the Bizet family finances, just as it affected the rest of Paris. His wife wrote at the time:

"We are not yet dying of hunger . . . I have not yet eaten cat, dog, rat or mouse, as is being done in even the best society: I shall taste donkey for the first time today!"

Once again, the Opéra-Comique presented Bizet with another libretto, *Djamileh*, and, following delay after delay, Bizet's corresponding opera was eventually staged in Paris on 22 May 1872. Despite the fact that the opera failed miserably at the box office, it did signal a change in Bizet's writing, and this was noticed by many, not least the composer Camille Saint-Saëns. It also became a favourite work of Gustav Mahler. The newly-changed compositional voice was also evident in another work written in 1871. Bizet wrote to a friend of *"the absolute certainty of having found my path"*, musically. The work he was referring to, from 1871, was *Jeux d'enfants*, (*Children's Games*). `recommended 3`

The year of 1872 was much like any other for Bizet – one of ups and downs. His son was born on 10 July and was christened Jacques. He also received another commission, this time for the theatre. There was to be a staging of a play by Alphonse Daudet, to be produced at the Vaudeville theatre in Paris, and it was Bizet's job to provide the incidental music. He produced some of his most endearing music to date, despite the fact that there were some difficult restrictions placed on him. Not least of these was that he could only write for 26 musicians. Bizet realised this was something of a challenge but decided not to compromise his compositional style. Possibly as a result, his incidental music was poorly received when the play was staged. Undeterred, Bizet immediately set about culling a small selection from it, and re-scoring the whole thing for a full orchestra. So it was that, only some six weeks after the play had failed, the new orchestral suite of the same music was performed to a rapturous reception. The suite and the play were both called *L'Arlésienne – The Old Woman of Arles*. `recommended 4`

In a letter to Bizet's friend in 1871 there is mention of *Jeux d'enfants*. The same letter also mentions a new three-act libretto, received from his relative and cohabitee, Ludovic Halévy. Along with it came a commission from the Opéra-Comique for a brand new opera. He went on to write: *"It will be gay, but with a gaiety that permits style."*

The work to which he was referring – as early as 1871 – was *Carmen*. It was based on a story by Mérimée, and, even in its slightly watered-down version as a libretto, it was always going to create problems with its audience, dealing out what was considered to be shocking realism for the time. There were also severe delays and difficulties with the management at the Opéra-Comique, and so the opera only received its premiere on 3 March 1875. Some critics attacked it for its *"lurid"* subject matter. Others attacked it because they supposed that Bizet had adopted the methods of Wagner. The public was not overly enthusiastic, either, although the houses were by no means disastrous. Financially, Bizet received 25,000 francs for the score from the publisher Choudens, so it was anything but a debacle for him, even if he was aggrieved at the work's reception. It had a run of 37 performances during the year and, of course, has become possibly the most popular opera in the world ever since.

recommended **5**

On the 33rd of those initial 37 performances, on 3 June 1875, Bizet died of a fever and a coronary attack. He was buried in Montmartre cemetery and it is said that, on the same night, the cast of *Carmen* could barely get through the opera, often weeping openly.

That's Bizet tallied. Musically, he was certainly not the most consistently successful composer ever, leaving a long line of half-finished works, together with many completed works which are never heard today. This mirrors his financial position, too, which was certainly up and down, though he was never destitute, despite living through the Paris Commune.

RECOMMENDED LISTENING

 SYMPHONY IN C
Scottish Chamber Orchestra/Jukka-Pekka Saraste

"AU FOND DU TEMPLE SAINT" FROM
THE PEARL FISHERS (*Arguably the most popular single piece of opera. The most celebrated version is sung by Jussi Björling and Robert Merrill*)
Jussi Björling/Robert Merrill/RCA Victor Orchestra/Renato Cellini

 JEUX D'ENFANTS
Toronto Symphony Orchestra/Andrew David

 SUITE NO. 1 FROM *L'ARLÉSIENNE*
Montreal Symphony Orchestra/Charles Dutoit

 "HABANERA", "SEGUIDILLA" AND "TOREADORS' SONG" FROM *CARMEN*
Angela Gheorghiu/Thomas Hampson/Orchestre National du Capitole de Toulouse/Michel Plasson

CHOPIN'S NOTES

Name:	Fryderyk Franciszek Chopin
Nationality:	Polish
Born:	1 March 1810

That's the same year that … P.T. Barnum was born

Died: 17 October 1849

The same year that … David Livingstone crossed the Kalahari

Wealth rating: £

Fryderyk Franciszek Chopin was born in February or March 1810, in the small village of Zelazowa, part of the Polish duchy of Warsaw. Chopin's French-born father was a tutor to the local nobleman – Count Skarbek – and Chopin's mother was Skarbek's housekeeper. The family were not particularly well off to say the least, Fryderyk being the second of four children. The finances probably took a turn for the better, though, when Chopin's father took up the post of lecturer in French and English at the Warsaw Lyceum, while at around the same time, the family began to take in boarders.

Chopin's musical nature was apparent from early on and it prompted his father to scrape together the necessary money to send the young Fryderyk for piano lessons – albeit with a mediocre local teacher. The lessons immediately highlighted the true nature of Chopin's genius and, by the age of nine, he had made his first public appearance, playing a piano concerto. When he was 11, the then celebrated singer Angelica Catalani heard him play and was so impressed she gave him an inscribed gold watch. At the age of 16, his keyboard skills led him to be picked to demonstrate a new instrument, the Aeolomelodikon, to Tsar Alexander the First, for which he received payment of a diamond ring.

Chopin was accepted at the Warsaw Conservatory when he was 17 and, although he received lessons in every aspect of music, his abiding love still remained the piano. He graduated three years later with distinction and the comment *"A musical genius"* on his final report.

In April 1829 Chopin's father was refused a government travelling scholarship for his son. So he decided that he himself had to fund a limited musical tour for Fryderyk. As a result, the composer visited Vienna, Germany and Italy, where his performances of his own early compositions – performances for which he was not paid, incidentally – were greeted enthusiastically. Success followed in his native Warsaw. Buoyed by it all, Chopin decided he would go to live in Vienna, to try to make money from his music. He took with him compositions such as his variations on Mozart's tune from *Don Giovanni*, "La ci darem la mano".

recommended 2

Despite a ringing endorsement from the composer Robert Schumann, who wrote *"Hat's off, gentlemen, a genius!"*, Chopin's time in Vienna proved unsuccessful and he was unable to interest either concert promoters or publishers. So he moved on to Paris, the city that was to become his home for the rest of his life.

Paris proved to be the making of Chopin. His very first concert there, where tickets were just ten francs, was a huge success. The great reviews that followed made Chopin quite literally an overnight sensation. He counted Berlioz, Liszt, Bellini, and Meyerbeer among his admirers and, possibly more importantly at the time, he attracted the attention of the Rothschild family. They soon became his patrons with the result that Chopin, from this point on, enjoyed total financial security, as well as entry, via his patrons, into the exclusive upper echelons of Paris society.

The new-found fame also meant that Chopin was in demand as a piano teacher. Ironically for someone who gave us so much piano recital music, he found playing for concerts *"distasteful"* and he used the Rothschild money to give it up. In fact, he hated playing in public so much that, during his lifetime, he only gave 30 public performances – a tiny number when compared to Mozart or Liszt, for instance.

As much as he hated public recitals, Chopin didn't mind teaching as a means of making extra money. In Paris in the 1830s, his stock was high, too. Around this time he was even more popular than Liszt as the Parisian piano teacher of choice. Chopin charged 20 francs – or 30 francs if he had to teach at the pupil's own house. Bearing in mind that 20 francs then was the equivalent to three times the average weekly wage and that Chopin had 150 to 200 pupils, then it's possible to see what a lucrative time this was for him.

Having said that, the cost of living the life of a composer was hugely expensive. Chopin once said: *"You probably think I'm making a fortune, but you're wrong. My carriage and white gloves alone cost more than I earn."* This is possibly the reason he was prone to signing himself *"Fryderyk Chopin, pauper"*.

Performing less and less in public meant that Chopin's reputation as a concert pianist began to fade. However, this was replaced by a growing reputation as a composer – a state of affairs which suited Chopin well.

The year 1836 saw the arrival in Chopin's life of Aurore Dudevant – better known as the author George Sand. It's fair to say that, at the time, Chopin was on the rebound. The parents of a girl with whom he was madly in love had forbidden their marriage on the grounds of ill health – Chopin's, that is. As a result, he was probably somewhat low when he received the amorous attentions of Aurore. The relationship did wonders for his composition and, following a rather fallow patch, he soon entered into a full nine-year period of great works.

Chopin and Dudevant holidayed together in Majorca, where Chopin's childhood tuberculosis recurred. Amazingly, when local people got wind of his illness, Chopin and Aurore had to retreat to a monastery at Valldemossa to avoid any undue, unfriendly attention. His beloved Pleyel piano was duly delivered, and it was here, holed up in the monastery, that he composed his 24 preludes. **recommended 5** He'd already received 500 francs for the preludes from the publisher Camille Pleyel. In addition, he had used them as equity, as it were, for a loan of a further 1,500 francs from his friend, the banker Auguste Léo.

Chopin was still only 26 years old and was financially doing pretty well. How do we know this? Well, he was already lucky enough to have enjoyed several fashionable addresses, living in what has been described as *"luxurious seclusion"* at addresses like No. 16, rue Pigalle and later No. 9, place d'Orléans. By 1836, though, it was a stylish, right-bank apartment in the rue de la Chaussée d'Antin and, when he ordered chic new furniture to put in it, the cost of it all, according to the composer Liszt, was already giving Chopin attacks of *"worry and nerves"*.

In 1841 and 1842, he took part in lucrative private concerts, the first of which earned him a staggering 6,000 francs. His chief form of income at this time was still his teaching. Although he was paid very well for his compositions, the commissions didn't come along all that often.

When his relationship with George Sand cooled, the effect on Chopin was startling. His interest in composing more or less ceased and his health went into further decline. He gave his last concert in Paris on 16 February 1848, aged 38. One week later, revolution broke out in Paris, and the knock-on effects for Chopin, as for many others, were disastrous. His teaching immediately dried up and so he decided to take up a long-standing offer from a wealthy Scottish pupil of his, Jane Stirling, to venture to Britain for a series of recitals.

When he got to England, he played at a number of private concerts for "the great and the good" – Lady Blessington, the

Duchess of Sutherland, even Queen Victoria herself. But the real point of his stay was the prospect of several public concerts in London, Manchester, Glasgow and Edinburgh.

As you can imagine, a schedule that took a man as ill as Chopin the length and breadth of England and Scotland, in the kind of transport available in 1848, was always going to take its toll. When he returned to Paris later the same year, he was no longer well enough to compose or to give lessons. He moved from a small apartment in the village of Chaillot – the rent of 400 francs half-funded by his friend, the Princess Obreskoff – into what would be his final address. No. 12, place Vendôme was wholly funded by a generous gift of money from the Stirlings, who had organised his British trip, and it proved to be a lifesaver: but not for long.

Chopin moved there in the autumn of 1849 and, at two o' clock in the morning on 17 October, he died, aged only 39. His funeral was attended by around 3,000 people and he is buried in the famous Père-Lachaise cemetery in Paris, where he now rests close to Jim Morrison and Edith Piaf.

RECOMMENDED LISTENING

 THE MINUTE-WALTZ *(even the fastest version in the Classic FM library of the Waltz in D flat – better known as the "Minute-waltz" – doesn't come in under a minute. Jean Yves Thibaudet takes 1 minute 35 seconds to play it. But who's counting?)*
Jean Yves Thibaudet

 VARIATIONS ON "LA CI DAREM LA MANO"
Emanuel Ax /Orchestra of the Age of Enlightenment/Sir Charles Mackerras

PIANO CONCERTO NO. 1
Martha Argerich/Montreal Symphony Orchestra/
Charles Dutoit

 ÉTUDE IN E (*TRISTESSE*)
Vladimir Ashkenazy

 "RAINDROP" PRELUDE
Evgeny Kissin

 PIANO CONCERTO NO. 2
Murray Perahia/Israel Philharmonic Orchestra/
Zubin Mehta

 PIANO SONATA NO. 2 IN B FLAT MINOR
(the "Funeral March" is its third movement)
Mikhail Pletnev

GRIEG'S NOTES

Name:	Edvard Hagerup Grieg
Nationality:	Norwegian
Born:	15 June 1843

That's the same year that ... Dickens published A Christmas Carol

Died:	4 September 1907

The same year that ... Picasso painted Les Demoiselles d'Avignon

Wealth rating:	𝕷𝕷

Edvard Hagerup Grieg was born on 15 June 1843 in the Norwegian town of Bergen. His father's side of the family had originally arrived in Norway from their native Scotland, where their name was Greig – with an ei, not ie – which would have been pronounced the Scottish way, sounding "greg". Grieg's father and grandfather were both British consuls in Bergen while his mother was the daughter of one of the province's governors.

Grieg was the fourth of five children and he soon showed musical leanings. He learnt piano from his mother from the age of six and took an active part in the many family musical gatherings. His first compositions date back to when he was around 15, which is around the time the family moved to his mother's estate at Landås, near Bergen.

The Norwegian composer Ole Bull attended one of the Grieg family music evenings and was extremely impressed by the young composer. Bull persuaded the Griegs to send their son to the Leipzig Conservatoire and, at the age of 15, Grieg began taking rather old-fashioned piano lessons with a pianist called Louis Plaidy. It was truly old-school teaching and Grieg asked for a different teacher. He was placed with a pianist called Wenzel, who had been good friends with Schumann and encouraged a lifelong love of Schumann's music in Grieg.

When he was 17, Grieg became unwell. It appears he had an attack of pleurisy, resulting in the removal of one of his lungs. He returned to Norway to recuperate before finishing his conservatoire course at the age of 19. Here, he presented the world with his opus 1, *Four Pieces for Piano*, and opus 2, *Four Songs*, as his graduation works.

Back in Norway, he began to play more of his own music in concerts, as well as standard repertoire concertos with orchestra. When he was 20, he applied for government money to take another period of study, but was refused. So he decided to move to Copenhagen, which was then the centre of not just Danish musical life but also Scandinavian music.

Grieg came under the influence of Niels Gade, the leader of the Danish romantic school, and a good friend of Schumann and Mendelssohn. Gade encouraged Grieg to write a symphony, which the composer duly did, although he was less than pleased with the result. The manuscript bears a hand-written note from Grieg, issuing instructions that the youthful work was never to be played. It was also around this time, aged 20, that Grieg met up with his cousin, Nina Hagerup, a talented singer, and within the year the two were engaged. Reports of her vocal abilities vary, but the composer Tchaikovsky would later say of Nina: *"I have never met a better-informed or more highly-cultivated woman."* There followed a flurry of songs to texts by Hans Christian Anderson, written specially for his new fiancée, called *The Heart's Melodies*.

recommended **1**

During the summer of 1864, the 21-year-old Grieg decided to stay with his original mentor, Ole Bull. Up until this point, Grieg's influences had been largely Danish, but this summer with Bull was going to change all that. He spent much of his time playing the classics and, for the first time, discovering something of the music and the culture of his native Norway. Later that same year, he met with the young Norwegian nationalist composer, Rikard Nordraak. Nordraak took Grieg into his lodgings where they spent the days and nights singing and playing – not only their own work but also Norwegian peasant music.

From this point on, Grieg dedicated his music to his country's nationalist cause. He co-founded the Euterpe Society for the promotion of Scandinavian music and began to incorporate Norwegian folk idioms into his music. With Nordraak, he planned to tour Germany and Italy, but Nordraak fell ill. Grieg went ahead with the planned trip, but on the way back to Norway via Berlin, Grieg received news that Nordraak had died. On 6 April 1866, Grieg finished a funeral march, dedicated to his late friend.

Back in Norway, he applied for the post of musical director at the Christiania Theatre – Christiania was the name of Oslo at that time. He was unsuccessful. Before leaving Christiania, Grieg gave a concert of Norwegian music which left him with a healthy 150 specie dollars in the bank. He also began to perform in public, often with his fiancée Nina, and when he was 23 his reputation as one of the country's leading musicians was sealed. As a result, he began to take on pupils. He applied for the job of conductor of the Philharmonic Society and won it.

On 11 June 1867, just a few days before his 24th birthday he married Nina. By the end of the year, his increasingly happy and comfortable circumstances had allowed Grieg to finish his first set of *Lyric Pieces*. **recommended 2** The couple had a baby daughter, Alexandra, and they soon decided to spend a couple of months in the milder air of Denmark and journeyed to Søllerød. It was during this particular holiday, with money beginning to be less of an issue and surrounded by his growing family, that Grieg wrote possibly his most enduring work, the Piano Concerto in A Minor. **recommended 3**

Once back in Norway, Grieg organised a series of lucrative subscription concerts. He also continued to petition the government for funds to subsidise more study and travel abroad.

The funds were eventually granted when Grieg was 26 and in 1869 he was able to set out for Italy with the help of a government stipend, probably to the tune of around 1,000 krone. The trip was no doubt partly intended as a way of getting away from recent domestic unhappiness: Grieg's daughter had died, aged only 13 months, and Nina had also later miscarried.

Between 1870 and 1872, Grieg cracked on with many Norwegian settings, and also wrote the stage music to Bjørnson's *Sigurd Jorsalfar*, premiered at the Christiania Theatre in May of 1872. He also made time to help found the Christiania Music Society for the promotion of orchestral music.

In the January of 1874, Grieg received a letter, inviting him to write the incidental music for a brand new play. It was a thorough letter, detailing exactly the music the author thought was needed at each point of the play. It ended: *"I will stipulate a royalty of 400 specie dollars, to be divided equally between us. Yours, very sincerely, Henrik Ibsen"*

COMPOSERS' NOTES NOTE

While writing *Peer Gynt*, Grieg said: *"I have written something for the [one] scene ... something that I literally can't stand to listen to because it absolutely reeks of cow turds, Norse-Norwegianness, and be-to-thyself Enoughness"* The particular part of *Peer Gynt* to which he was referring was "In the Hall of the Mountain King". **recommended 4**

Although he had been working on an opera with Bjørnson, Grieg accepted the commission immediately, stopping work altogether on his previous project. The Ibsen play in question was *Peer Gynt*. However, the work took Grieg much longer than he expected. Fortunately, around the same time, he had received yet another government stipend. This one, sought in conjunction with Ibsen, was to the tune of 1,000 krone and allowed Grieg the freedom to continue the work on *Peer Gynt* in peace. Grieg travelled to Denmark and then to Leipzig, where he finished the score in the July of 1875. It was performed the following year.

Throughout 1877 and 1878, Grieg rented lodgings at Lofthus in the beautiful Hardanger district of Norway, and spent an extended period composing, surrounded by nature. Ill-health prevented him from writing much at all for a further year or two, but his international reputation continued to grow.

By 1880, aged 37, he was composing once again, mainly new songs. He also became conductor for his native Bergen Harmonic Society for a couple of years, the last official post he would ever hold. When this came to an end, he was able to start a second piano concerto, commissioned by the music publishers Edition Peters in 1883, for which he was to be paid the sum of 3,000 marks. It would never be finished. He did, though, complete a cello sonata and a second set of *Lyric Pieces* for Edition Peters.

Grieg's was marriage under strain, and in 1883 he left Nina. He was also unhappy with his composing. Nina moved in with friends, who tried desperately to reconcile the couple. In the end, they succeeded and the Griegs were reunited in Leipzig in 1884, before spending four months in Rome.

Back in Norway, and somewhat happier, Grieg wrote the "Holberg Suite" – or to give it its correct title, *From Holberg's Time* – for the 1884 Holberg bicentenary being celebrated in Bergen. Grieg also composed two other works for the Holberg festivities – *Album Leaves* and *Improvisations on Norwegian Folk Songs* – the proceeds from both of which he donated towards a fund to build the Holberg statue in Bergen. He also built himself a house in Troldhaugen, where he lived from April 1885 until the end of his life.

For the next 20 years or so, Grieg settled down to a yearly routine. He composed in the spring and early summer; in the late summer, he would go walking in the mountains, often with friends (one of those friends being the composer Percy Grainger); autumn and winter were spent abroad, on concert tours, chiefly to earn money but also to spread his music and make sure his international reputation remained undiminished.

In 1887, Grieg met Frederick Delius, who was then studying in Leipzig. He was very impressed with Delius and did all he could to encourage him to continue. A year later, Grieg met Delius's father while on a concert tour of England. Delius's father was intent on putting a stop to his son's musical career but, under pressure from Grieg, was persuaded to change course and allow his son to become a composer. The mutual admiration these two composers held is reflected in a little-known fact – the main tune from Delius's piece, *On hearing the first cuckoo in spring*, is not a Delius original: it is actually a folksong arranged into the music. Delius had taken the song from Grieg's 1896 arrangements of *19 Norwegian folk tunes*.

In the late 1890s, when Grieg was in his fifties, he rediscovered his Norwegian nationalism afresh in song cycles, miniatures for orchestra and more *Lyric Pieces*. He celebrated his 25th wedding anniversary, whereupon Edition Peters sent him a silver bowl filled with gold pieces. He was also given numerous awards and prizes, including honorary doctorates from Cambridge and Oxford, as well as membership of the Institut de France. In 1898, he was the driving force behind the Norwegian Music Festival in Bergen.

His vociferous condemnation of the Dreyfus affair (the political scandal which rocked France at the end of the 19th century) led him to cancel a French tour in 1899. When he finally agreed to go to France again in 1903, he had to travel with a police guard. It may be one of the reasons that his working relations with French musicians were not good, and why, in a newspaper review of Grieg's music, the composer Claude Debussy described the Norwegian's music as *"pink bon-bons, filled with snow"*. Another highlight of this time was being visited in Bergen by Kaiser Wilhelm II in 1904, with whom he is said to have talked nothing but music and religion.

This was also the time of the Edvard Grieg Fund, set up by Grieg and 50 Bergen businessmen. Each of the 50 men wrote codicils into their wills bequeathing 25,000 krone to the Grieg Fund on their deaths; a total of 1,250,000 krone. Among other things, it was the Grieg Fund in 1906 that raised the 100,000 krone to build a new public library in his native Bergen. It also made the formation of the Bergen Philharmonic Orchestra financially possible.

Grieg's last composition was written in 1906 – the *Four Psalms*. During the winter of 1906 to 1907, his health became a major cause for concern. In search of a better climate, he moved into a hotel in Christiania but, even then, continued to tour to Copenhagen, Munich and Berlin. On 3 September, he was on the point of setting off on an English leg of his tour when his doctors ordered him to hospital. He died the following day. His funeral was a national event, on a scale not seen in Norway before – 50,000 people lined the streets. His ashes were sealed into a specially-hewn rock recess, overlooking the fjord at Troldhaugen. The Griegs' house in Troldhaugen was sold at auction and the money given as a further bequest to the Bergen Public Library.

Today, Norway could not be more proud of its number one musical asset. Much like the English are able to see Elgar on the back of a £20 note, so the Norwegians see Grieg on a 500 krone note.

RECOMMENDED LISTENING

"TWO BROWN EYES" AND "I LOVE YOU" FROM *THE HEART'S MELODIES*
Anne Sofie von Otter/Bengt Forsberg

LYRIC PIECES
Geir Henning Braaten

 PIANO CONCERTO IN A MINOR
Leif Ove Andsnes
Berlin Philharmonic Orchestra/Mariss Jansons

 "IN THE HALL OF THE MOUNTAIN KING" FROM *PEER GYNT*
Gothenburg Symphony Orchestra/Neeme Järvi

BOCCHERINI'S NOTES

Name:	Ridolfo Luigi Boccherini
Nationality:	Italian
Born:	19 February 1743

That's the same year that ... US President Thomas Jefferson was born

Died:	28 May 1805

The same year that ... Thomas Jefferson was elected for a second term

Wealth rating:	🏛🏛🏛🏛

Ridolfo Luigi Boccherini was born in the Italian town of Lucca on 19 February 1743. His father was a singer and double-bass player with the local church music group, the *Capella Palatina*, and the family's income was not poor but certainly modest. It was a very artistic family environment: Boccherini's brother became a poet and librettist, working with the composers Salieri and Franz Joseph Haydn, while two of his sisters became famous prima ballerinas and another became an opera singer. Boccherini himself was taught music first by his father at home and, at the age of eight, attended the Seminario di San Martino in Lucca. Here he was given a thorough musical training by the maestro di capella, Domenico Vannucci. Significantly, Vannucci, as well as being a music tutor, was also a top-class cellist, and Boccherini soon took up the cello himself, something he fitted in between singing in the church choirs of Lucca.

When Boccherini was ten years old, he was shipped off to study in Rome, where the then famous Costanzi was his teacher. Again, significantly, Giovanni Costanzi's nickname was "Giovanni del Violoncello" – a sort of "Joe the Cello" – and so the cello became even more important in Boccherini's musical life. Indeed, he eventually made his public debut on the instrument at the age of 13 in Lucca, playing a cello concerto. It is said that, even at this early stage, Boccherini was commanding huge fees which has led some scholars to conclude that he was already a supreme cellist. He made his Viennese debut aged 15, after which point Boccherini and his father were given jobs as musicians at the Viennese Court Theatre, the Kärntnertortheater. Boccherini enjoyed a few successful seasons in Vienna, all the time continuing to travel to play in Italy: one concert in Florence, when he was 18, describes him as the *"celebrated cello player"* and, importantly, reports that the compositions of his own were *"d'un maniera dell tutto nuova"* – of a completely new kind. Boccherini, the composer as well as the cellist, appears to have made his first impression.

In 1764, when Boccherini would have been 21, he was appointed as cellist back at the Capella Palatina in Lucca, a job he combined with composing. A year later, he was to be found performing at what are described as *"well-paid concerts"* in Cremona, Pavia and Rome. When his father died in 1766, Boccherini was 23, and he upped sticks to Genoa, where he was able to pick up several high-profile noblemen as patrons before embarking on a mini tour, which took in Nice and Paris.

In Paris, Boccherini was again able to engage patronage, this time of the wealthy Baron de Bagge. At least two of Boccherini's works had been published in Paris before he arrived there, suggesting that his name as a composer was now beginning to surpass that as a cellist. While in the French capital, he also published his *Six Keyboard Sonatas*, and was able to sell numerous copies and editions, as well as giving many performances in the well-to-do salons.

From Paris, Boccherini moved on to Madrid, having apparently been promised a job there by the Spanish ambassador to France. Eventually, by 1768, when Boccherini was 25, he was playing in the orchestra of an Italian opera company in Aranjuez. Some of Boccherini's music at the time was dedicated to Prince Carlos of Asturias, who was the patron of the opera company. Incidentally, anyone watching the 2006 film of the life of Casanova should look out for Boccherini. It appears that Boccherini visited Valencia with his Italian opera company and there met the famous Giacomo Casanova. He is even mentioned in Casanova's *The Story of my Life* as the *"célèbre Boccherini"*.

In 1770, at the age of 27, Boccherini married one of the sopranos in his opera company, the delightfully-named Clementina Pelliccia. They went on to have six children. The same year, he also landed a new job as *"compositore e virtuoso di camera"* for the infant Don Luis – the king's brother – in Aranjuez, on a salary of 14,000 reals: that's something like the equivalent of £28,000 today. This was a very well-paid position in late-18th-century terms and Boccherini's compositional style began to show signs of this more comfortable existence. He began composing for different instruments and in different genres, completing six symphonies within a year. The fact that Don Luis had an existing string quartet meant that Boccherini could join them on the cello, enabling him to write pieces for the relatively new medium of string quintet with two cellos.

COMPOSERS' NOTES NOTE

From the neck of the Don

Boccherini's boss, the infant Don Luis, had an allergy which meant that he couldn't wear any clothing close to his neck. As a result, portraits of Don Luis – probably the most celebrated being by Goya – always show him with weird, plunging necklines, totally out of keeping with the fashion of the day.

All seemed to be going well and in 1772, at the age of 29, Don Luis increased Boccherini's salary to 18,000 reals, or around £33,000 by today's standards: he was clearly valued and appreciated by Don Luis. When the Don moved first to Talavera, then to Cadalso de los Vidrios, and finally to the Sierra de Gredos – the vast mountain range which borders the plains of Castille – he took Boccherini with him.

While in the Sierra de Gredos mountains, Boccherini turned his thoughts to business. He was taken on by the celebrated Viennese publisher, Artaria, despite the distance from his current home to Vienna. He also began petitioning for composition commissions with one of the crown princes of Prussia, Crown Prince Wilhelm. Indeed, he was so successful that his existing boss, Don Luis, quickly decided to increase his pay in order to keep him. According to his new contract, dated 17 August 1784, Boccherini received an extra 12,000 reals – around £23,000 – bringing his salary now to 30,000 reals, or around £56,000.

In 1785, when Boccherini was 42, his wife, Clementina, died. Her death was followed closely by that of Boccherini's patron, Don Luis. Instantly, he was left without a salary. He quickly wrote a petition to King Carlos III, who granted him an annual pension of 12,000 reals – that's around £23,000: quite a step down from the previous £56,000 but nevertheless an amount of money which was to last the rest of his life. He was promised the next cello job that came up with the Capilla Real – the Chapel Royal – and, within just a couple of years, a position arose. Nevertheless, Boccherini's earnings were now seriously diminished. He looked through his notes and dug out the address for Crown Prince Wilhelm. By a stroke of luck, the prince had recently had a major promotion. He was no longer plain old Crown Prince Wilhelm: he was now King Friedrich Wilhelm II, and he immediately gave Boccherini a new job, as *"compositeur de notre chamber"* on a salary of 1,000 Prussian thalers – that's something like £25,000 today. As a result, from that point on, Boccherini supplied the king with 12 instrumental works a year, probably from his base in Spain.

In March 1786, when he was 43 years old, Boccherini was also employed as *"director de orquesta y compositor"* by the Duchess of Osuna. Osuna was a famous music patron of her day and she paid Boccherini 1,000 reals per month for his work. So, if we add it all up, Boccherini was on: 12,000 reals from King Carlos,

1,000 thalers from King Wilhelm and 12,000 reals from the Duchess of Osuna. That's a modern-day total of around £71,000: not a bad turnaround for someone who was unemployed and without salary just a year earlier.

In 1787, Boccherini was 44. He remarried, to Maria del Pilar Joaquina Poretti, the daughter of a cellist at the Capilla Real. When King Carlos III died in 1788, his son Carlos IV continued Boccherini's pension. Boccherini in turn probably wrote for some of the new chamber music groups established by the new king.

In 1796, when Boccherini was 53, his daughter Joaquina died, aged just 25. The same year, he entered into an agreement with the Paris publisher, Pleyel, for the sale of 58 works for the sum of 7,200 reals – around £10,600. A year later, Boccherini's patron, King Friedrich Wilhelm, died, forcing Boccherini to re-petition yet again for his employment. This time, the application was refused. Immediately, Boccherini lost his 1,000 thalers per year. As a result, it appears that Pleyel may have taken advantage of the composer's needy situation when it came to his next agreement – the sale of 110 works, but for just 9,600 reals: that's around £14,200.

Shockingly for Boccherini, the Duchess of Osuna then decided to stop her patronage in 1799, which meant that the composer was now another 12,000 reals a year down on his regular salary.

True to form, despite Boccherini's hard times, his popularity saw him turn the situation around again. His works had always been popular in France, particularly in Paris – he had even dedicated his six recent piano quintets to *"the French nation"*. He turned down an invitation to be on the board at the Paris Conservatoire, and acquired a new French patron – the French ambassador to Madrid, Lucien Bonaparte. In 1802, with Boccherini aged 59, Bonaparte granted him a pension of 3,000 francs per year – or around £7,000 today – a timely intervention which saw Boccherini if not comfortable then at least surviving once more.

Sadly, Boccherini's three daughters and his second wife then all died within a couple of years and many said that this hastened Boccherini's own death. Those who came to visit him in these later years were said to have found him living in his one-room apartment, in a state of near-permanent exhaustion. By 1804, he had more or less given up composing and was living a very modest life indeed, all the while his health deteriorating. He died of tuberculosis on 28 May 1805 and was buried in the church of San Justo y Pastor in Madrid. Later, in 1927, his remains were taken to Lucca where he was re-buried in the basilica of San Francesco. Despite living such a modest existence towards the end, his will does show that he owned not one but two Stradivari cellos. Ironically, one of these alone would sell today for around £2.1 million.

COMPOSERS' NOTES NOTE

In just the same way that Mozart has K numbers – K for Köchel, the man who numbered all Mozart's works – Boccherini has G numbers. It seems Boccherini made a catalogue of all his own works, but that these were all destroyed in the Spanish Civil War – along with a large number of Boccherini manuscripts. In 1969, as man first stepped on the moon, Yves Gérard completed a new numbered catalogue of Boccherini's music. Hence, the G numbers – the *Stabat Mater* is G532, for example.

RECOMMENDED LISTENING

MINUET FROM THE STRING QUINTET IN E
Capella Istropollitana

CELLO CONCERTO NO. 7
Yo-Yo Ma/Amsterdam Baroque Orchestra/Ton Koopman

CELLO CONCERTO NO. 9 IN B FLAT
Jacqueline du Pré/English Chamber Orchestra/ Daniel Barenboim

SYMPHONY NO. 3 IN C
I Solisti Veneti/Claudio Scimone

STABAT MATER
King's Consort and soloists/Robert King

GERSHWIN'S NOTES

Name:	George Gershwin (Jacob Gershovitz)
Nationality:	American
Born:	26 September 1898

That's the same year that ... Zola wrote his "J'accuse" letter

Died:	11 July 1937

The same year that ... Vanessa Redgrave born

Wealth rating:	£££££

George Gershwin was born as Jacob Gershovitz on the 26 September 1898 in Brooklyn, New York, to Russian immigrant parents. His dad, Morris, was a minor-level entrepreneur who was by no means rich. When George was 12 years old, Morris brought a piano into the family home, intended for George's brother, Ira. It was soon clear that George was going to monopolise the instrument, though. A year later, he embarked upon his first formal musical training, taking lessons from a well-known New York teacher at the time, Charles Hambitzer. Luckily for the Gershwins, the lessons came free – simply because Hambitzer enjoyed teaching him so much.

It was around this time, when he was just 13 or 14, that George started work. He began doing fairly long hours after school in his father's restaurant for just $4 per week, while still practising the piano in any spare moment. At 15, he left school and headed for Tin Pan Alley – the general name for the business area of New York devoted to music publishing. Back then, music publishers would employ entire offices full of pianists to play their new songs so that people might buy the sheet music. George got a job with one such publisher, Remicks, where he was paid $15 per week – a sum which must have seemed like heaven to a 15-year-old schoolboy. It's said that, from this point on, Gershwin started to keep a book of his ideas for songs, labelled with the letters G.T. – which stood for Good Tunes.

He quickly became recognised as a fine pianist, and one who could improvise brilliantly. To earn extra money, he gained a moonlighting job with the Standard Music Roll Company in East Orange, New Jersey, playing music for the big thing of the time – Piano Rolls. This brought him $35 for every session of around six songs. Bearing in mind that the average weekly wage in the US at the time was around $15 per week, you can see why he went on to cut around 140 piano rolls in the following ten years.

On 17 March 1917, George left his job with Remicks and auditioned for the great contemporary songwriter and director Sigmund Romberg. Romberg was immediately impressed and took Gershwin on to help write his next Broadway musical. He did a stint, too, as a staff composer at Harmes Music Company. Here he was on $35 per week, plus a $5 advance and three cents for royalties on any of his tunes that were published. It was while he was here that his first big break came. He wrote a song with a wordsmith called Irving Caesar, which they soon pitched to Al Jolson. Jolson put it straight into his new show, *Sinbad*, and it became the hit song of the show with the sheet music selling more than two million copies. In its first year alone it earned Gershwin around $10,000 in royalties. The song was *Swannee*. Gershwin had arrived.

He was now able to give up playing for piano rolls and concentrate on the things he really wanted to do. And what he *wanted* to do was, ironically, write *serious* music. So when, in late 1923, aged just 25, the bandleader Paul Whiteman approached him with the vague idea of writing a "jazz concerto", George eagerly, if idly, agreed. When he heard nothing more on the subject from Whiteman, he promptly forgot about it and carried on with his song writing.

It came as a shock to Gershwin when, in January 1924, he saw an ad for a rather eclectic concert that was to include a new jazz concerto by . . . himself. The ad said that the concert was to be on 12 February – Gershwin had around one month to write the work. Yet write it, he did. He handed the completed piano score to Whiteman's arranger, the composer Ferde Grofé, who orchestrated it. Gershwin had written it for Whiteman's band at the time, hence the reason for the famous opening slide on the clarinet, which still foxes some players today: this was a particular trick which Whiteman's clarinet player, Russ Gorman, had perfected, and so it had been written into the music.

COMPOSERS' NOTES NOTE

Compose yourself . . .

It's said that Gershwin approached Ravel, asking for composition lessons. Ravel responded by asking how much Gershwin had earned that year. *"Around $100,000!"* answered Gershwin. *"Well,"* said Ravel, *"it is you who should be giving me lessons!"* The story is also told with Gershwin asking the same question of Stravinsky, and with a figure of $250,000, so you'll have to make up your own mind about its veracity.

In the audience at New York's Aeolian Hall for the premiere were none other than Jascha Heifetz and Sergey Rachmaninov. On the rather eclectic bill were both Edward Elgar's *Pomp and Circumstance* march and *Yes, We have no Bananas.* Nestled in at the end of the night, was the new "jazz concerto" by George Gershwin, entitled *Rhapsody in Blue*, with Gershwin himself playing the solo piano part. Imagine what it must have been like to hear that Russ Gorman slide on those opening bars for the first time. It's said that, on the night, Gershwin was embellishing and improvising his own score wildly, and that, instead of using printed music, he simply nodded the orchestra back in after each of his piano sections. **recommended 1**

A year after *Rhapsody in Blue*, Gershwin found himself very much in the big time. He was brushing shoulders with Alban Berg in Vienna, as well as Maurice Ravel, and Igor Stravinsky in Paris.

Gershwin was now being approached with all manner of offers for new works, while at the same time keeping up his lucrative song composing for shows. It was a letter, though, from the conductor Walter Damrosch that stood out from the rest. The New York Symphony Society – of which Damrosch was principal conductor – wanted to commission a concerto from Gershwin. He couldn't resist, and he had pretty soon finished what many believe to be his finest orchestral work, the Piano Concerto in F. **recommended 2**

Gershwin was now 28 years old and in huge demand. He was writing songs still as if they were going out of fashion, but was also ever on the hunt for a more serious stimulus. It was probably around this time that he read a book called *Porgy* by DuBose Heyward, a writer from Charleston, South Carolina. Gershwin was smitten with the book and wrote to Heyward immediately, suggesting a collaboration. It's a measure of his success at the time that when Heyward said yes to the project, the next free time that Gershwin could find in his schedule to work on it was eight years later in 1934.

In the meantime, Gershwin made tours of Europe, as well as moving to Hollywood for a short time in 1930, under contract to Fox Studios. By this time, he'd also completed a new work which had been premiered two years earlier by the New York Philharmonic Orchestra. He had drawn out the ideas while he was in Paris on tour, and finally completed the orchestration in Vienna. It was called *An American in Paris* and it is said to describe his own view of Paris: its sights and sounds. **recommended 3**

The year 1931 dawned and Gershwin came up with his musical *Of Thee I Sing*, something which stands out in the Gershwin catalogue for a number of reasons. Firstly, it won him a Pulitzer

Prize, the first musical comedy ever to win one. But, more importantly, as regards George and his money, it was to be his last big success in the theatre. He wrote two sequels in 1932 and 1933 but they both flopped. From this point on, Gershwin would succeed now in the cinema and with his more serious works. Even here, though, it wasn't all plain sailing. He tried to repeat the success of *Rhapsody in Blue* with a new piece – the *Second Rhapsody* for piano and orchestra, written for the Boston Symphony Orchestra. This, too, fell into obscurity.

A holiday in Cuba in 1932 led to him writing the exuberant *Cuban Overture*, and it was in 1934 that he finally settled for the summer in Folly Beach, Charleston, with his brother Ira and the writer DuBose Heyward, to write the long awaited *Porgy*. *"If I am successful,"* Gershwin wrote at the time, *"it will resemble a combination of the drama and romance of* Carmen *and the beauty of* Meistersinger.*"*

The new work, now entitled *Porgy and Bess*, tried out at the Colonial Theatre in Boston on 30 September 1935 and then transferred to the Alvin Theatre in New York, where it ran for a disappointing 124 performances. It was not until years later that the people who put up the backing for the show made any returns on their investment and, even then, *Porgy and Bess* was never *truly* successful in Gershwin's own lifetime. Even now, it is still probably more successful in Europe than it is in its native US. Its first staging at the Metropolitan Opera House was a full 50 years after the premiere. **recommended 4** and **recommended 5**

Some critics have claimed that *Porgy and Bess* is a flawed opera: more a collection of good songs than an opera. Gershwin himself, not surprisingly, was dismissive of this notion. *"I am not ashamed of writing songs at any time, so long as they are good songs. Most of the successful operas of the past have had songs. Nearly all of Verdi's operas contain what are known as 'song hits'.* Carmen *is almost a collection of song hits."*

In his last years, Gershwin went back to Hollywood again, where he was a fully-paid-up member of the musical aristocracy. It's funny to think, now, but it's said that he would often play tennis with the atonal composer, Arnold Schoenberg.

In 1937, Gershwin began work on music for a new movie, *The Goldwyn Follies*. He soon started to complain of headaches, but doctors found nothing. He blacked out on stage on 10 February that year. On 9 July, he played the piano in the morning but was in a coma by the end of the day. It was decided that he needed immediate surgery, but America's top brain surgeon was on holiday on his yacht. It says something about Gershwin's status that President Roosevelt himself sent two US navy destroyers to fetch the surgeon. It was too late. He died from a brain tumour on 11 July 1937, at the age of only 38. As he said to his sister in his last few weeks: *"I haven't yet scratched the surface in music."*

Despite successfully crossing over into the world of classical music, Gershwin made his real money from his songs. If you think that *Swanee* made him $10,000 in its first year, and that he wrote hundreds of songs, many much more successful, then it is easy to see how he became a staggeringly wealthy man. Among the many hundreds of songs he wrote, many with his brother Ira, you can find some great titles. Personal favourites include the clearly romantic *Blah Blah Blah* and the somewhat cerebral *I'm a poached egg, without a piece of toast*.

As well as this, Gershwin made money from concert fees and royalties, not to mention his weekly radio show. He was an ardent art collector and left a serious collection on his death. When the famous Forbes Rich List compiled their list of 19 of the highest-earning dead celebrities, it included both Cole Porter and Richard Rodgers. Gershwin wasn't on the list, they pointed out, but he almost certainly would have been if they could only find out how much he earned for the Gershwin estate.

That's Gershwin – one of the most financially successful composers ever.

RECOMMENDED LISTENING

 ### *RHAPSODY IN BLUE*
Howard Shelley/Philharmonia Orchestra/Yan-Pascal Tortelier

 ### CONCERTO IN F
Howard Shelley/Philharmonia Orchestra/Yan-Pascal Tortelier

 ### *AN AMERICAN IN PARIS*
Pittsburgh Symphony Orchestra/Andre Previn

 ### "SUMMERTIME" FROM *PORGY AND BESS*
Ella Fitzgerald/Louis Armstrong/Russell Garcia

 ### "BESS, YOU IS MY WOMAN NOW" FROM *PORGY AND BESS*
Ella Fitzgerald/Louis Armstrong/Russell Garcia

DVOŘÁK'S NOTES

Name:	Antonín Dvořák
Nationality:	Bohemian
Born:	8 September 1841

That's the same year that ... Sir Robert Peel became prime minister

Died:	1 May 1904

The same year that ... Theodore Roosevelt was elected US president

Wealth rating:	£££££

Antonín Dvořák was born on 8 September 1841 in Mulhausen, not far from Prague, in what was then Bohemia. His father was a butcher, albeit a musical one: he could play the zither quite well and would often play for family parties. Although Dvořák's father recognised Dvořák's musical side early on, he allegedly insisted that his son learn the butcher's trade too. Indeed, in one of the enduring mysteries of Dvořák's life, there exists a certificate which states that Antonín Dvořák has taken the necessary steps to qualify as a butcher. The only problem is . . . it's a fake – and a late fake, at that.

In fact, his father let him pursue a musical career with the proviso that he must at least learn a musical *trade* so that he would be able to earn a living. Dvořák chose to be an organist and, at the age of 12 years, was sent away to study – financed not by his father but by a rich uncle. During this time, as well as organ, he learned piano and viola.

After graduating from organ school at the age of 20, he attempted to find a job as an organist, but posts were few and far between. This was the start of a 12-year period of fairly stark poverty. To make ends meet, he turned to his viola to gain employment in a fairly smalltime private orchestra, run by a conductor named Karel Komzak. The orchestra eked a living playing waltzes, polkas and light medleys, both in restaurants and for weddings. Eventually, he found himself playing in the orchestra of the Prague National Theatre. During all his time as a viola player, his annual salary peaked at 348 gulden – that's around £2,800 today. Dvořák was now 25 years old and the conductor at the time in the National Orchestra was the composer Bedřich Smetana. Smetana, already a more respected figure, was himself paid between 1,200 and 2,000 gulden – £9,000 to £16,000 today. Amazingly, Dvořák stuck at the theatre job for 12 years, much of the time secretly composing but not daring to show anyone his work.

After 11 years in the pit, he gave up his salary of 348 gulden to be the organist at the church of Saint Adalbert in Prague. The salary was 138 gulden or £1,200, so this was not a great move financially but one which gave him the chance to devote much more time to composing. To supplement the tiny salary, he took on piano pupils and, as was often the way with these great composers, fell in love with one of them.

The name of his love was Josefina Čermáková, but she did not return his affections. Dvořák switched his amorous allegiances to her sister, Anna Čermáková. This proved to be a much more reciprocal arrangement and the Dvořáks were married in the November of 1873. Dvořák would have been 32 years old. Immediately short of money, they moved in with her parents, but then set up a very modest home in an apartment in Prague just a few months later.

Dvořák's income at this time was still from organ playing and giving piano lessons, but his composing was definitely beginning to come out of the closet. His opera *King and Charcoal Burner* made it onto the rehearsal schedules at the National Theatre, although it eventually proved to be too ambitious for the cast and musicians, and was dropped. At this point Dvořák, burnt a number of his early works – *"my mad period"*, as he called it – but then coolly and pragmatically began his personal opus numbering again from scratch. Significantly, his choral work *Hymnus* was performed in 1873, and he was immediately hailed as a new and important composer. During the next couple of years, his reputation grew and in 1875 he was awarded an annual grant of 400 gulden from the Viennese ministry of culture – the equivalent of around £3,700 now. Although still a modest sum, Dvořák was buoyed and the money enabled him to increase his composition rate. One of the most successful pieces to come from this period was his *Serenade for Strings.* **recommended** *1*

That same year, Dvořák felt confident enough financially to move to a better apartment in Prague, and for a while the family was happy. Tragically however, that same year Dvořák's baby daughter, Josefa, died. He poured his and his family's grief into a new choral work. He set the popular words of a mediaeval poet, Jacopone de Todi, set often before, famously by Pergolesi and Rossini. The *Stabat Mater* concerns the mother of Jesus, standing at the foot of cross, grieving for her child. Dvořák's blossoming as a composer, combined with his personal situation at the time, produced a powerful setting which, still today, vies for supremacy with the two earlier works. He included the piece in a submission for a renewed grant in 1876 and was awarded the sum of 500 gulden – around £4,400. **recommended** *2*

Dvořák celebrated his 36th birthday in 1877 and he won an important financial boost from an unexpected source. In the course of his successful submissions for grants to the Viennese ministry of culture over the previous few years, Dvořák had to submit a number of his own pieces. On the board of the ministry was the composer Johannes Brahms, and Brahms was beginning to be quite taken with Dvořák's work. So much so that in 1877 – when along with another application, Dvořák submitted his *Moravian Duets* – Brahms had a bright idea. He would recommend Dvořák to his publisher, a man called Fritz Simrock – then *he* could pay Dvořák for his new works. So he wrote:

"With regard to the state stipend, for years, now, I've been enjoying the music of Antonín Dvořák from Prague. This year, he sent these ten duets for two sopranos, and they seem a very good proposition for publishing. Play them through, and see if you like them as much as I do . . . He's a very talented man, and, moreover, he's poor. Think about it!"

There's nothing like a good word. It did the trick, too. Simrock, though, didn't pay Dvořák for the *Moravian Duets*, reminding Dvořák that he was unknown in Germany, the most important musical market at the time – and nor did he pay him for his next work, the *Slavonic Dances Book 1*. **recommended 3** Dvořák was unconcerned, though. He was being published and getting his music and his name out there. Soon the tide would turn in his favour.

For Dvořák, the 1870s were just one decade-long upward curve, both musically and financially. The *Slavonic Dances Book 1* was a publishing success – phenomenon, even – and Simrock straight away asked for an orchestral arrangement, for which he *did* pay: 150 gulden or around £1,300. The financial stability allowed Dvořák to move to a larger apartment – in the same block, incidentally – which would become his permanent Prague home. It also meant that he was able to support his father, who had been forced to give up his job and was eking out a living as a zither player.

Dvořák's ongoing publishing deal meant that his music was now being heard in Dresden, Berlin, Vienna and as far afield as

COMPOSERS' NOTES NOTE

Humorescape

Legend has it that the great violinist, Joseph Joachim, was wandering around Dvořák's flat one day, looking for music to play. *"Have a look in that old box,"* shouted Dvořák. *"There's loads of stuff I've never had published in there."* Joachim looked into the rather scruffy trunk, picked a manuscript out and began to play it. The scrappy piece of paper would go on to become one of Dvořák's most enduring works – *The Humoresque*. It is so "public domain", in fact, that it has its own set of slightly rude words. Only space prevents them from being printed here, of course.

recommended 4

Budapest, Lugano and even America. His international success fostered an increased reputation in his native Bohemia and he rapidly became the musician of choice when commissioning Bohemian music for state occasions – pieces like his *Festival March* for Emperor Franz Josef's silver wedding, and the *Prague Waltzes* for a state ball.

Back to finances and the future looked rosier by the day. Simrock paid him the equivalent of £4,400 for his violin concerto and a huge £17,000 for both the *Hussite Overture* and a piano piece for four hands. The success gave Dvořák increasing confidence to challenge his publisher. When the Royal Philharmonic Society commissioned Dvořák's seventh symphony, his publisher offered him around 1,500 gulden for it – that's around £16,000. Dvořák wrote him a polite letter:

"If I give you my symphony for 1,500 gulden, then I'll have lost another 1,500 gulden – because other firms have offered me 3,000 gulden for another publishing deal. And for that I don't need to supply a symphony – just a few songs here and there . . . piano pieces or whatever . . . Please remember, I'm a family man and a poor artist!"

I think Dvořák is going a little easy on the truth in his description of himself. By this time, he was by no means a starving artist. He was clearly a shrewd businessman who, in the end, achieved his asking price of 3,000 gulden for the seventh symphony – that's around £32,000.

One morning in 1891, in his Prague flat, Dvořák opened a telegram from America. It was from New York and it contained an offer of work. If Dvořák was to agree to go to New York to teach, for just eight months of each year, they would put on ten large concerts of his music per year. The offer was tempting: and so too was the money at 30,000 gulden – or £300,000 for the eight months' work. At first, Dvořák turned it down. Only after the persistent intervention of the US millionaire, Jeanette Thurber, did he agree. He landed in New York on the steamship

Saale in late September 1892, and soon made his home on East 17th Street, with handsome views of Stuyvesant Park.

Teaching duties apart, his new riches and wealthy lifestyle now allowed him the financial freedom to compose what he wished. He soon started work on a new symphony, infused with some of the styles and shades of America. It's important to note, at this point, that his New World Symphony contained *"not one tune"* he didn't compose himself. As he said:

"It is the spirit of Negro and Indian melodies which I was striving to reproduce . . . I have not used a single one of them: I've simply written characteristic themes, imbued with Indian music." **recommended 5**

Dvořák spent two years in America and was back in Prague by 1895. By then, his American years and the profits from his many English tours meant he'd been able to buy a single-storey barn from his brother-in-law, which he then had converted into a country dwelling. His publisher gladly snapped up three symphonic poems for 6,000 gulden – that's around £60,000, and quite a difference from his first pieces which brought him just 150 gulden. Two years later, he was asked to sit on the board of the Viennese ministry of culture – the same board to which he had applied as a struggling composer some 22 years earlier. He was made director of the Prague Conservatory in 1901 and appointed to the Austrian House of Lords.

Musically, he turned to the world of Czech legend for his inspiration and specifically to opera, which he thought was the easiest way to reach the highest number of people through music. Now very comfortably off, he was able to spend almost a year on the libretto of a young poet, Jaroslav Kvapil, for the Prague National Theatre. It was Dvořák's most artistically successful opera to date, *Rusalka*. **recommended 6** Unfortunately, it never received its planned Vienna premiere, which would have been under the baton of Vienna Opera director, Gustav Mahler, mainly because Dvořák wanted too high a fee.

Dvořák spent the last years working on an opera, *Armida*, which would prove nowhere near as successful as *Rusalka*. When Dvořák died, on 1 May 1904, he was a rich man and his death was marked by a national day of mourning.

RECOMMENDED LISTENING

 SERENADE FOR STRINGS
Bavarian Radio Symphony Orchestra/Sir Colin Davis

 "TUI NATI VULNERATI" FROM *STABAT MATER*
Chorus of the Dresden State Opera/Staatskapelle Dresden/Guiseppe Sinopoli

 SLAVONIC DANCE IN C FROM THE *SLAVONIC DANCES BOOK 1*, OP. 46
Chamber Orchestra of Europe/Nikolaus Harnoncourt

 HUMORESQUE
Maxim Vengerov

 SYMPHONY FROM THE NEW WORLD
Berlin Philharmonic Orchestra/Claudio Abbado

 "SONG TO THE MOON"' FROM *RUSALKA*
Renée Fleming/London Symphony Orchestra/Sir Georg Solti

HAYDN'S NOTES

Name: Franz Joseph Haydn

Nationality: Austrian

Born: 31 March 1732
That's the same year that … Covent Garden Opera House opened

Died: 31 May 1809
The same year that … Charles Darwin was born

Wealth rating: £££££

Franz Joseph Haydn was born in Austria on 31 March 1732. He was the second of 12 children, only six of whom would survive into adulthood. Haydn's family were not well off at all and, as far as is known, the Haydns had no great musical tradition. Apart from a vaguely musical uncle, Haydn's dad had taught himself to play the harp by ear, but that's where it ended. After a spell with his uncle – in which a thrashing was more commonplace than a good meal – he entered St Stephen's Cathedral in Vienna as an eight-year-old boy soprano. Many stories survive of Haydn's schoolboy pranks during these "treble" years – swinging from the scaffolding, singing deliberately out of tune, even cutting off a fellow singer's pigtails.

In those days, a cathedral choir could be quite a ruthless affair: as a boy soprano, if your voice broke, it often meant you were broke, too. Haydn found himself on the street at the age of 16, with only *"three wretched shirts and a worn-out coat"* to his name. He was forced to share lodgings with a friend, the delightfully named Michael Spangler, a small-time singer and music teacher.

Haydn eventually borrowed enough money to move out and rent an attic room which contained, as he put it, *"an old worm-eaten"* clavichord. He might have been poor but at least he could practise. More importantly, he could earn money through teaching, too.

"For eight long years," he said, *"I was forced to knock about wretchedly, giving lessons to the young!"* He also sang in choirs and played for weddings, funerals and baptisms. He then became the valet and factotum to the composer Nicola Porpora, polishing shoes and cleaning clothes in exchange for the odd composition lesson. It seems odd to think of the great Haydn blacking boots, but Haydn himself took it in his stride.

Before long, he was spotted by an Austrian count, Maximilian von Morzin, who took him on as his music director at his family estate in Lukavec. It was his first real job, which gave him 200 gulden per year, plus free board and lodgings. This was a perfect starter job for Haydn – it gave him a manageably-sized orchestra, and meant he was able to spend the winters with the Count in Vienna, which he loved.

Haydn's first symphony was written when he was 27. When he was 28, he got married. He had been in love with one of his Viennese pupils for a good few years. When, in 1760, she announced she was to become a nun, Haydn did what he thought was the honourable thing at the time – he married her sister.

His new wife, Anna Maria, was, by all accounts, a bit of a beast. She was uncultured, unfeeling and she had no interest in Haydn's music whatsoever. The stories about her lack of appreciation of the great composer are legion but my favourite has got to be the time he came home and found that she'd lined her pastry tin with one of his manuscripts. They eventually agreed to live apart and, although he sent her money every month, Haydn allegedly never opened a single one of her letters.

He'd been married just a year when his employer, Count von Morzin, let go of the orchestra and its musical director, Haydn. Luckily for Haydn, though, Prince Paul Anton Esterházy came to hear that he was out of work. He offered Haydn the post of assistant Kapellmeister at his estate in Eisenstadt, 30 miles outside Vienna. Haydn would remain in service to the Esterházy family for the rest of his long life.

In the Esterházy household, Haydn became an assistant to the old and frail figure of composer Gregor Werner. Werner was earning a very respectable 400 gulden per year – that's the equivalent of around £10,000 today, and commensurate with a composer of some experience and standing. Tellingly, Haydn was immediately placed on the same salary, and promised he could have the top job as soon as it became free.

Fascinatingly, Eisenstadt records reveal that Haydn was also paid a further sum of 200 gulden. So the new assistant was on 600 gulden compared to the boss's stipend of just 400 gulden – or £15,000 compared to £10,000 in today's money. Eventually, when Werner was told about the extra money, he didn't like it and he developed a hatred of Haydn that would manifest itself in numerous written complaints to the boss. They were all to no avail.

For his money, Haydn had to compose, and conduct two operas and two concerts per week, as well as provide daily chamber music. When Paul Anton died and Nicholas the Magnificent took over, music became even more important. Nicholas entertained on a big scale and nowhere more so than in his personal 400-seat theatre.

In 1766, when Haydn was 34, Werner died, giving Haydn total control of the music, including the right to write the church music – something which went with the top job. Also, Nicholas moved his summer residence to his Esterházy palace, at Süttör in Hungary. Esterházy had its own marionette theatre, its own opera house and, very soon, its own purpose-built theatre. The only problem for Haydn was filling all these venues with music.

Eventually, the work rate took its toll on him. He performed 125 concerts and staged 17 operas in 1786 alone. Legend has it that he wrote the new Nicholas a symphony, designed to tell him that he and the musicians needed a holiday. In it, Haydn had each player leave the stage, one by one, so, at the end, it was eventually only Haydn conducting a lone fiddler. We need a break, was the message. Apparently, it worked. The symphony was his number 45, which is now generally called the "Farewell".

recommended 1

Three years later, Haydn's salary was increased to 961 gulden 45 kreuzer – that's around £24,000 today and the third highest salary on the entire Esterházy estate. In 1779, he renegotiated his contract with the publisher Artaria and he won back the rights to his own work from Prince Nicholas. From 1780 to 1790, both Haydn and Artaria made a great deal from his music: precisely how much is hard to say, but it probably put his standard salary very much into perspective.

In 1790, Prince Nicholas – Haydn's long-time champion – died, to be succeeded by his son, Paul Anton II. Paul Anton II disbanded the orchestra and disbanded the choir. Haydn, though, was kept on, on a wage of 1,000 gulden, but with effectively no job to do. So what did he do?

He travelled. First of all, he spent time in Vienna, which he loved. Then he took up an offer of a man called Johann Peter Salomon who was a sort of Raymond Gubbay of his day. Salomon invited him to visit London and cash in on his fame by playing in concerts. Haydn agreed and signed on the dotted line to conduct 20 concerts, each to include a premiere. He received £300 for six new symphonies, plus a further £200 for their copyright. There was to be £200 for his participation and another £200 guaranteed for a benefit performance.

The tour proved to be a huge success, and three years later Haydn did it all again. This time, his reputation was even greater than before, due to his previous visit. He played by royal command 26 times for King George at Carlton House and Buckingham Palace. King George asked him to stay on in England – he even offered him a suite of his own rooms at Windsor Castle. Haydn seriously considered the proposition, but eventually turned it down – possibly something to do with the English fogs, which played on his rheumatism. He was summoned back to Esterházy – but not before cheekily putting in a bill to Buckingham Palace for his so-called "command performances". The bill was for 100 guineas, which the palace duly paid.

COMPOSERS' NOTES NOTE

Haydn wrote his Symphony No. 94 for London, for a concert in the then-famous Hanover Rooms in London's Hanover Square, just off Regent Street. He was paid handsomely for these concerts but one thing still annoyed him. The noble women who attended would often have had a rather good dinner prior to the performance and, amid the hot, stuffy atmosphere of the non-air-conditioned rooms, they would often nod off to sleep. Hence, Haydn wrote his Symphony No. 94, the "Surprise" Symphony, with its unexpected loud chords at the beginning, to wake them from their slumbers. That was in 1795. Some 202 years later, Classic FM moved into new studios, just 100 yards from Hanover Square – the birthplace of the "Surprise" Symphony.

 recommended 2

Before he left, he gave another benefit concert, which included his Symphony No. 104, the "London" Symphony. That one night alone brought in the equivalent of around £100,000 today! Not bad for a night's work. In all, this particular tour ended with a clear profit of £2,000, money which was to make him comfortable for the rest of his days – that is, if he wasn't already.

Back in Esterházy, Paul Anton II had now died, to be replaced by his son, another Nicholas. Nicholas wanted to revive the famous Haydn orchestra and Franz Joseph readily agreed, and promptly treated himself to a brand new house in the suburbs of Vienna. This was also the time that he supplied the Viennese trumpeter, Anton Weidlinger, with a brand new trumpet concerto to show off Weidlinger's flash, new modern trumpet of 1796. **recommended 4**

By 1796, Haydn was well and truly back home from London. Nicholas the Second had by now abandoned Esterházy and so Haydn was back to wintering in Vienna and summering in Eisenstadt. As he was Kapellmeister, he now wrote all the Esterházy church music and was obliged to write a mass each year for Nicholas's wife, Princess Maria, which he duly did.

It was this new-found choral duty, combined with the fact that he'd heard a great deal of Handel's oratorios in London, that made him set his sights on writing his own oratorio. In 1796, he started out on a setting of both the words from Genesis and Milton's *Paradise Lost*. He then got a group of Viennese aristocrats to agree to sponsor a private performance of the new work, each guaranteeing Haydn the sum of 2,250 gulden. That's around £60,000 each. The oratorio was a resounding success, and is still considered to be his finest choral work today. It was called *The Creation*. **recommended 5** Just a couple of years later, he pulled off another coup with another new oratorio, *The Seasons*. It was sponsored by local dignitaries in much the same way as *The Creation* had been, with a premiere given at the Viennese Imperial Palace in 1801. **recommended 6**

In 1802, Haydn's health was failing him and he resigned from his job as Kapellmeister. Nicholas the Second, while accepting his resignation, insisted on him staying at Eisenstadt and raised his annuity to 2,300 gulden, plus all his medical bills were paid. At a time when pensions were totally discretionary, this was an amazing figure.

Haydn made his last public appearance in 1808, in a concert conducted by Salieri, in which he had to be helped on to the stage. When, in 1809, Napoleon attacked Austria, bombarding the outskirts of Austria for a full 24 hours, Haydn refused to leave. As a result, Napoleon had a guard of honour placed around Haydn's house, for protection. Nevertheless, it is often said that the bombardment, going on all around him, used up the last of his energies. He died in his sleep on 31 May 1909 – the music at his funeral was by Mozart.

As composers go, Haydn has got to be one of the most successful. He got recognition in his own lifetime and down the ages. And that would be that if it weren't for one thing – a fascinating financial fact to take to your next dinner party. Haydn was given a talking parrot when he was in England which, upon his death, was sold at auction. Because it was Haydn's parrot, it fetched 1,400 gulden – that's more than £35,000 today. For a parrot! Even in death, Haydn was worth a fortune.

RECOMMENDED LISTENING

"FAREWELL" SYMPHONY (NO. 45)
The English Concert/Trevor Pinnock

"SURPRISE" SYMPHONY (NO. 94)
Capella Istropollitana/Barry Wordsworth

CELLO CONCERTO IN D
Steven Isserlis/Chamber Orchestra of Europe/
Roger Norrington

TRUMPET CONCERTO IN E FLAT
Wynton Marsalis/English Chamber Orchestra/
Raymond Leppard

"THE HEAVEN'S ARE TELLING THE GLORY OF GOD" FROM *THE CREATION*
Chicago Symphony Orchestra and Chorus/Sir
Georg Solti

THE SEASONS
Freiburg Baroque Orchestra/RIAS Kammerchor/
René Jacobs

MEYERBEER'S NOTES

Name:	Giacomo Meyerbeer (Jakob Liebmann Beer)
Nationality:	German
Born:	5 September 1791

That's the same year that … The Observer was founded

Died:	2 May 1864

The same year that … Tolstoy started writing War and Peace

Wealth rating:	£££££

First of all, let's get his name straight. On 5 September 1791, Jakob Liebmann Meyer Beer was born. The Meyer and the Beer were separate, being the family names of his mother and father respectively. So, originally, his name was simply Jakob Beer. He was born in Berlin, into a rich, German-Jewish line. His father was a wealthy industrialist who often worked to contracts from the Prussian Army while his mother was from a wealthy banking family.

Jakob took piano lessons early on – Clementi was one of his teachers – becoming a classic composer prodigy by the age of 11. When he was 14, he began composition lessons and at 19 he left home to take up extended studies with the well-known Abbé Vogler in Darmstadt. Alongside him in Vogler's classroom was the composer Carl Maria von Weber, who went on to become a lifelong friend. By now, Jakob had started the practice of combining his mother's name with his father's – Meyer and Beer together – but his first name was still, at this point, Jakob.

An early oratorio, *Gott und die Natur*, was a favourite of the Grand Duke of Hesse and Jakob was appointed to the position of court composer at the age of 20. It was also around this time that he composed his first opera, *Jephthas Gelübde*, staged in Berlin in

1812. Despite this and other early operatic successes, he was still known at this stage chiefly as a pianist – in fact, possibly the best of his day.

When Meyerbeer was 23, he moved to Paris to further his musical education. It was to prove an important move. Meyerbeer loved Paris, not only making the most of all it had to offer in itself, but also using it as a base for other European visits. He came to London to hear some of the great pianists in concert. When he was 25, he visited Italy. Although this latter trip was meant to be a short study tour, it ended up lasting nearly ten years. The Italian period was, like Paris, to prove a crucial one. It was here that he really began to compose opera in earnest – and where he changed his name one final time. In deference to the country where he appears to have found himself, musically speaking, he decided to change his first name to its Italian form: Giacomo Meyerbeer.

Out in Italy, he was given his first job. He set the work of an Italian librettist in Padua, Gaetano Rossi, and the resulting opera, *Romilda e Costanza*, brought him some success in Padua and round about. Meyerbeer had a practice of writing for specific singers, which continued in his next opera, *La Semiramide riconosciuta*. This was written for Turin and tailored for the then famous alto, Carolina Bassi Manna. Although this made for a more or less perfect opening night, she was granted exclusive rights of performance in the part. When she opted not to take up these rights, the opera was subsequently little performed.

Meyebeer's next venture was for Venice. With another libretto by Rossi, Meyebeer had a triumph with *Emma di Resburgo*. It was premiered when Meyerbeer was 27 and the critics loved it. As a result, it was taken up by opera houses all over Europe, helping to spread the Meyerbeer name far and wide. His friend, the composer Weber, staged the work in Dresden, and it was also performed in Vienna, Budapest and Warsaw. His next work, for La Scala Opera House in Milan, was *Margherita d'Anjou*, and the demanding La Scala audience approved. His fees for writing *Emma* and *Margherita*? Absolutely nothing. He merely retained rights and was able to choose librettists and cast singers. *Margherita* was a huge hit and soon played to full opera houses around Europe. Meyerbeer had definitely arrived.

On 7 March 1824, at the age of 32, Meyerbeer premiered his latest opera, *Il Crociato in Egitto*, in Venice. It confirmed his place as the most important composer of Italian opera after Rossini. By now, Paris had truly woken up to the phenomenon of Meyerbeer. Ironically, it was Rossini who first staged *Il Crociato in Egitto* in Paris, followed by *Margherita*. The French opera goers began to itch for Meyerbeer operas: Meyerbeer himself knew the importance of the Paris opera market and began to sketch out several possible projects which might be suitable for his grand assault on the capital. When he was 35, he was finally commissioned to write a three-act comic opera for Paris. It was the moment he had been building towards.

Sadly, though, Meyerbeer's father had died just a year earlier and, as new head of the family, he also had to apply his thoughts to "the family line". He married his cousin, Minna Mosson on 25 May 1826. It was to prove a close marriage, with five children, although his wife's often poor health meant he frequently travelled alone to his professional engagements. The year 1826 also saw the death of his friend, the composer Weber, at the age of only 40, and Meyerbeer is said to have been seriously affected by the loss. Work on his planned Paris opera was temporarily put aside. Meanwhile, in 1829, Rossini staged his new opera, *William Tell*, in Paris, and many considered it a giant leap forward.

Meyerbeer eventually focused on his work for Paris. It was called *Robert le Diable* recommended 2 and it was eventually premiered in 1831 and was the biggest spectacle of its day. It not only made a fortune for its composer but also for the Paris Opera House itself, grossing upwards of four million francs at the box office in its lifetime. That's the equivalent of £5 million across a lifetime today. Before the end of the 19th century, the Paris Opera alone had performed the work a staggering 756 times.

Within a year of its Paris premiere, the libretto of *Robert le Diable* had been translated into virtually every European language. Meyerbeer visited London in 1832 to oversee the British premiere, staying at the Waterloo Hotel in Jermyn Street, which was at the time listed as a *"central house, chiefly for bachelors"*. It appears the English capital, in general, though, was not to his liking:

"The climate does not agree with my stomach," Meyerbeer wrote home, and *"in this famously clean and comfortable London I have been so badly lodged, so dirtily and uncomfortably, that in three days I've twice changed hotels . . . the cooking doesn't suit me either, and neither does the beer!"*

COMPOSERS' NOTES NOTE

Getting composers' goats

It is said that, having moved to Paris, Meyerbeer was working one day on his operas, but struggling to concentrate due to an organ grinder playing outside his window. Worse still, the musician was playing nothing but the tunes from Rossini operas, driving Meyerbeer to distraction. Meyerbeer sent his servant to give the man four francs – that's around £50 today – to go and play Meyerbeer tunes under *Rossini's* window. The servant returned minutes later but the musician was still playing. *"He says Rossini has paid him eight francs to play here for you,"* the servant allegedly reported.

Buoyed by the enormous success of *Robert le Diable*, Meyerbeer agreed to write a new opera, based on the 1572 St Bartholomew's Day massacre. Differences with the librettist, Eugene Scribe, led him to break off his contract, and he was forced to pay a penalty of 30,000 francs – that's around £50,000 today. Eventually, work restarted on Scribe's libretto, and the penalty fee of 30,000 francs was repaid in 1834. The new opera, *Les Huguenots* **recommended 3**, was premiered on 29 February 1836. The composer Hector Berlioz said that Meyerbeer had packed the work with enough musical riches to fill 20 operas.

Within just one and a half months of the first night, the work had taken 11,300 francs at the box office, a sum never achieved before in such a short period of time – that's worth around £30,000 today. It became the most successful opera of the 19th century, and the first to receive a thousand performances at the Paris Opera. To this day, that record has only been beaten by Charles Gounod's *Faust*. It is often said that part of Meyerbeer's success was down to him using his wealth wisely – he would not shy away from spending large amounts on the publicity for his operas, in much the same way as musicals do today.

Although now positively bathing in success, if Meyerbeer faced any problems at all it was simply what to do next. He had taken drama and scale to such a height in *Robert le Diable* and *Les Huguenots* that his only danger was of falling victim to his own standards. Nevertheless, he began work on his next subject, *Le Prophète* **recommended 4** as early as 1841, when he was 50. He lodged his first version of the opera with a legal notary in Paris but, such was the scale of Meyerbeer's search for perfection, the work's first night was only in 1849, with the alto heroine's role played by legendary singer Pauline Viardot, in what was to become one of the great alto roles in all opera.

Le Prophète was the first opera to employ the amazing spectacle of the electric spotlight, built specially for the performance by the famed physicist, Foucault. It is important to remember that this was 1849, and the electric spotlight literally dazzled its first-night audience. This was the same first-night audience which was also confronted with an amazing denouement, in which an explosion kills everyone on stage. At the time of the premiere of *Le Prophète*, with not only its amazing new score but also its hi-tech staging, even Wagner was moved to say it was *"the prophet of the new world"*.

In 1842, Meyerbeer had been made Generalmusikdirektor in Prussia. Up until this point, German composers and writers had no copyright protection. In 1842, the Hamburg Stadttheater tried and failed to introduce a system of royalty payments. Just a year later, Meyerbeer started his own system of payments at the Berlin Opera which allowed authors to receive a percentage of the ticket sales. This pioneering work on composers' rights as well as the Prussian job took up much of Meyerbeer's time until 1846, when he took leave of absence. Eventually, he resigned as Generalmusikdirektor two years later, though stayed on as director of Prussian court music.

In 1851, Meyerbeer began working once again on a subject he had been keeping in his bottom drawer. Entitled *L'Africaine* recommended **5**, it was a project he had started and put away as early as 1843. He revised the score before abandoning it yet again in 1853. It was all of seven years later when he began work on it again. However, this was interrupted by the death of his librettist, Scribe, in 1861. Further interruptions were to come. Meyerbeer travelled to London in 1862 to oversee the performance of his *Overture in the Form of a March* at the International Exhibition. During his visit, he stayed at The York Hotel in Albemarle Street, run by a Mr Crawley. At that time, Albemarle Street was considered one of the best – if not *the* best – streets for hotels in London, and the average price of a first-class room was around five shillings.

Meyerbeer eventually completed his opera in the November of 1863. In the time since his last major opera, *Le Prophète*, Meyerbeer had written a couple of smaller works for the Opéra-Comique: *L'Étoile du Nord* and *Le Pardon de Ploërmel*. *L'Africaine* went into rerheasals at the Paris Opera in the November of 1863. Meyerbeer died during rehearsals on 2 May 1864. He was aged 72. The opera eventually received its premiere in April 1865 – a full two years later and 22 years after Meyerbeer had originally begun work on it. Despite the fact that it lasted around six hours at its premiere, it was a phenomenal success.

That's Meyerbeer tallied – an extraordinarily successful and wealthy composer in his day, and who knows: perhaps ripe for a huge comeback anytime now.

RECOMMENDED LISTENING

 LES PATINEURS (*a ballet suite made up of Meyerbeer's music, but arranged by Constant Lambert*)
Philadelphia Orchestra/Eugene Ormandy

 ROBERT LE DIABLE
International Orchestra of Italy/Bratislava Chamber Orchestra/Renato Palumbo

 "NOBLES SEIGNEURS" FROM *LES HUGUENOTS*
Jennifer Larmore/Orchestra of the Welsh National Opera/Carlo Rizzi

 "THE CORONATION MARCH" FROM *LE PROPHÈTE*
St Louis Symphony Orchestra/Leonard Slatkin

 "O PARADISO" FROM *L'AFRICAINE*
Placido Domingo/Los Angeles Philharmonic/Carlo Maria Giulini

LISZT'S NOTES

Name: Franz Liszt

Nationality: Hungarian

Born: 22 October 1811
That's the same year that ... the Luddites destroyed industrial machinery

Died: 31 July 1886
The same year that ... the English Lawn Tennis Association was founded

Wealth rating: £££

Franz Liszt was born on 22 October 1811 in Raiding, near the Hungarian town of Odenberg. Both his father and his grandfather were land stewards for Prince Nicholas on the Esterházy Estate. Liszt's father, Adam was also a good musician, who played the cello in the Esterházy court orchestra – which means, incidentally, that Liszt's father would have played under the composer-conductor Haydn in his time. Who knows – maybe he was one of those string players who agreed to walk off the stage in the first performance of Haydn's "Farewell" Symphony? What is certain is that Liszt was born into a family with a fairly low yet secure wage.

Liszt was drawn to the piano at a very early age and, by the time he was nine years old, he was not only able to play extremely difficult concert-level pieces in public, he could also improvise on themes provided by his audience – something in which the young Mozart had specialised. By the age of ten, news of Liszt's virtuosity had reached Prince Nicholas. When the prince eventually heard Liszt play, he got together a group of Hungarian aristocrats and encouraged them to fund Liszt's musical education to the tune of 600 gulden per year – that's equivalent to £3,200 today. This gave him access to some of the finest music teachers of the time, based in Vienna: Mozart's great rival, Salieri, was his composition tutor. Some of Liszt's teaching came free of charge: the composer and pianist Carl Czerny – a piano-technique master – refused to accept payment, saying that the pleasure of teaching this amazing pupil was recompense enough. As a result, Liszt was soon heard on the concert platform, although not yet a teenager. Beethoven attended one recital where Liszt is said to have played an arrangement of Beethoven's Piano Trio – from memory – which elicited a kiss and a comment of *"Devil of a fellow!"* from the great man.

At the age of 12, Liszt left Vienna, bound for Paris, intent on a course of study at the Paris Conservatoire. But the director of the conservatoire at the time was the composer Cherubini, and he had other ideas. Cherubini was known to harbour a dislike of child prodigies, seeing them as a modern malaise. As a result, Cherubini enforced the rule – a rule that could be dropped in the right circumstances – that the conservatoire didn't admit foreigners. Liszt was refused entry and so was forced to resort to private tutors again, this time in Paris.

Paris was perhaps the ideal city from which to launch his career and in March 1824, at the Paris Opera, Liszt's debut French concert established his reputation virtually overnight. It wasn't only the audience that was wowed, either. It's said that when Liszt played a concerto that night, even the orchestra stopped playing in order to listen to him. From then on, Liszt had European salons at his feet and, by the still tender age of 16, was famous across the continent. More importantly, he was financially independent, having made so much from his concert performances. Sadly, his father, Adam, died the same year and Liszt was forced to become the family's sole breadwinner. The gruelling concert schedule which Liszt tried to maintain to provide for his family soon took its toll. He was eventually forced to cease his touring.

He took a few years off, opting to catch up with areas of his education which he had missed out. Financially speaking, this was probably the hardest time of Liszt's life. As a measure of how tight it became for him, he was forced to sell one of his most prized possessions – his beloved Erard piano. On a positive note, though, he read virtually everything he could lay his hands on. And he had the first of his many love affairs – on this first occasion with the 16-year-old daughter of the French minister of commerce, a relationship which was quickly extinguished by the girl's father.

Aged 19, Liszt encountered three composers who were to alter the course of his life. They were Fryderyk Chopin, Hector Berlioz and Niccolò Paganini. From Chopin, Liszt is said to have learnt the art of the refined salon style. From Berlioz, it was his ability to handle an orchestral palette when composing. It is perhaps from Paganini, though, that the most lasting effect on his style emanated. Paganini's stage presence and dazzling virtuosity deeply impressed Liszt and set him on a regime of practice that was to change not only his own life, but the way in which people thought about the piano for years to come. Between 1831 and 1833, Liszt virtually shut himself away, combining endless hours of practice with the constant stimulation of books. As he said:

"Homer, the Bible, Plato, Byron, Hugo, Beethoven, Bach, Mozart, Weber – they are all around me. I study them, meditate on them, devour them with fury. Besides this, I practise four to five hours of exercises. Provided I don't go mad, you will find an artist in me."

When he felt ready, Liszt launched himself back on the concert-going public – and the response was amazing. His technique now swept all other pianists aside. Apart from playing works by the great composers with a fury and effortlessness that was unmatched, the public was overawed by his fantasy compositions: huge, showman-like semi-improvisations on opera themes. The conductor, Charles Hallé, wrote of one performance:

"Liszt was all sunshine and dazzling splendour, subjugating his listeners with a power that none could withstand. For him, there are no difficulties of execution."

When he was 23, Liszt met and fell in love with the Comtesse Marie d'Agoult – a married woman with three children, who soon reciprocated his feelings. Within a year of their meeting, she had moved out of the family home and set up house with Liszt, far away from any whiff of scandal, in Geneva. They would eventually have three further children together, the second of whom, Cosima, would go on to marry the composer Richard Wagner. D'Agoult's personal wealth provided Liszt with a very timely financial safety net, allowing him to embark upon serious composition. One of the massive works he produced in the ensuing period was his epic *Années de pèlerinage – Years of Pilgrimage.* **recommended 1**

Despite going through both very lean and very wealthy periods, many records attest to Liszt's generosity. In 1838, for example, he undertook a series of concerts in Vienna – an entire season, at a typically punishing pace. When it was complete, he had made around 24,000 gulden. That's not a small sum – it's around £140,000 today. The money was not for himself, though – the series had been organised in order to donate the entire profits to the appeal for victims of the Danube Flood Disaster. Liszt didn't see a penny.

Between 1839 and 1847, when he was between the ages of 28 and 35, Liszt toured the concert platforms of Europe relentlessly, mixing with royalty and amassing a huge fortune in the process. But not all of it was for himself. When, in 1839, a campaign to raise money for a permanent memorial to Beethoven stalled, Liszt stepped in with a personal injection of cash from his own funds, enabling the project to be completed. It still stands today, in Bonn.

On other occasions, he appears to have helped many individuals. He gave the Swiss composer Joachim Raff a personal allowance of 600 thalers per year from his own pocket, plus full board and lodgings at Liszt's home. The allowance alone is the equivalent of £3,300 today.

In 1840, Liszt undertook a tour of the British Isles, promoted by the entrepreneur and conductor Louis Lavenu. The extensive list of dates was badly promoted and Lavenu lost around £1,000 – some £58,000 today – on the whole venture, and Liszt's fees were never paid. It would be a full 45 years before he was prepared to risk venturing to these shores again. Thankfully for him, this was just one upset in what was one of the most successful periods of concert touring by any composer, either before or since.

At the age of 35, Liszt changed direction once more. By this time, his relationship with Marie d'Agoult had virtually disintegrated. Liszt moved out and took his three children with him, returning to Paris, where he moved in with his mother. A string of mistresses followed, most famous among them were Marie Duplessis – who was eventually immortalised by Verdi as the "fallen woman" of his opera *La traviata* – and the dancer Lola Montez. The one lasting relationship he formed around this time was with the Polish-born princess, Carolyne Sayn Wittgenstein. This cigar-smoking intellectual was to prove Liszt's last great love, and the two shared their mutual interests of religion and mysticism. She was married but eventually left her husband – and his 30 or so servants – to join Liszt, who was by now living in Weimar.

In Weimar, Liszt became Kapellmeister to the Grand Duke and, during the next 13 years, he established the Weimar court as one of the chief artistic centres in Europe. As conductor, concert-season programmer and, of course, composer, he presented a huge range of forward-looking music as well as helping to enhance the reputation of some past great composers. It was also around this time that he courageously championed the work of the then disgraced and exiled Wagner, staging the first performances of *Tannhäuser* and *Lohengrin*. As he wrote to Wagner at the time: *"Your Lohengrin will be given under conditions that are most unusual and most favourable for its success. The directors will spend on this occasion almost 2,000 thalers on the production – a sum unprecedented at Weimar within memory of man."* The sum of 2,000 thalers is the equivalent of around £12,900 today.

Liszt's championing of Wagner would eventually be to his own detriment. When the Grand Duke refused to fund further performances of Wagner's other works, Liszt left.

Despite Liszt's devotion to Wagner and others, this was a fertile period for Liszt's own composing, too. During his Weimar years, he produced a huge amount of work: 12 symphonic poems, the *Faust Symphony*, the great B minor piano sonata and the *Totentanz* – the *Dance of Death* for piano and orchestra – as well as two piano concertos. **recommended 3**

At the age of 50, Liszt travelled to Rome with the intention of having the Pope sanction a marriage to Princess Carolyne, but this came to nothing. He decided to stay on in the Italian capital, and soon found himself attracted to something completely different – the religious life. When he was 54, Pope Pius IX conferred

COMPOSERS' NOTES NOTE

One of Liszt's pupils, pianist Carl Tausig, was a phenomenal keyboard player and also an infamous practical joker. It appears that Tausig took Liszt's manuscript score of his *Faust Symphony* and sold it – for just five thalers. Not long after, Tausig was packed off to study with Wagner instead.

on him the title *Abbé* and, although he was never fully ordained, he did receive the four minor orders in 1879.

In his sixties, Liszt divided his time between his life as an abbé in Rome, his piano teaching in Pest – which was later to combine with the adjacent city Buda, to form Budapest – and Weimar, to where he had been invited back just a couple of years earlier. In this period, Liszt was considered something of a "grand old man" of classical music, with composers from all walks of life sending him piano music to play, and an endless line of musicians begging him to attend their concerts. The letters Liszt wrote from this period number hundreds. Interestingly, many of the people he mentored in piano received his tutelage free of charge and his generosity became famous.

One of his final triumphs, at the ripe old age of 75, was a trip to England. Despite the fact that he was a little infirm and suffering from dropsy, he wowed people in a series of public concerts, as well as playing for Queen Victoria at Windsor Castle. From here, he travelled on to Bayreuth, for the music festival of his protégé and son-in-law, Wagner. While at Bayreuth, during a performance of *Tristan und Isolde*, he was taken ill. On 31 July 1886, he died, his last word said to be simply, *"Tristan"*.

RECOMMENDED LISTENING

 "THE BELLS OF GENEVA" (SUISSE) FROM THE *ANNÉES DE PÈLERINAGE*
Stephen Hough

 HUNGARIAN RHAPSODY NO. 2 IN C SHARP MINOR
Berlin Philharmonic Orchestra/Herbert von Karajan

 PIANO CONCERTO NO. 1
Joseph Banowetz/Slovak Radio Symphony Orchestra

 UN SOSPIRO
Van Cliburn

 LIEBESTRÄUME NO. 3
Van Cliburn

SCHUBERT'S NOTES

Name:	Franz Peter Schubert
Nationality:	Austrian
Born:	31 January 1797

That's the same year that…Samuel Taylor Coleridge wrote Kubla Khan

Died:	19 November 1828

The same year that…The Spectator was founded

Wealth rating: 💷

Franz Peter Schubert was born on 31 January 1797 in Vienna. The family was not rich by any means – Schubert's father was a schoolteacher. As a result, Schubert gained free lessons without having either to pay or even to leave the house. His father also taught him violin, and his elder brother taught him piano. Soon, though, it became apparent that Schubert needed more than in-house music tuition and he began lessons with the organist at the local parish church. Again, as is so often the case with many of the great composers, Schubert quickly outgrew these classes, too. At the age of 11, he was accepted as a choir boy in the court chapel, giving him automatic admission to one of the best boarding schools in Vienna, the Stadtkonvikt. Tutors at the school included the composer Salieri, and it wasn't very long before Schubert was not only leading the school orchestra but often conducting it. His first compositions date from his time at the Stadtkonvikt, including his first song, *Hagars Klage*.

When he left school in 1813, Schubert bowed to pressure from his father and initially agreed *not* to pursue a career in music. He went to teacher-training school and then took up the post of assistant teacher in his father's school. He did, however, continue to compose in his spare time. And, like many at the time, he began to read Goethe's *Faust*. His setting of part of it, when he was aged just 17, is generally considered to be his first masterpiece. *Gretchen am Spinnrade*, written in 1814, covers the section where Gretchen is sitting at her spinning wheel, thinking of Faust. **recommended 1**

Between the ages of 17 and 20, Schubert continued teaching by day and composing by night. He made friends with the extensive circle of poets and musicians in Vienna, people whose names are possibly now a little less familiar to us, but whose roles in helping Schubert develop were crucial. People like Johann Mayrhofer, a minor Viennese poet, provided the texts for many of Schubert's songs (often known by the German word, Lieder). Mayrhofer was a frequent guest at the many musical evenings, which were nicknamed "Schubertiads" because the composer himself always provided the music. Often, he would not only premiere his latest songs with his friend, the baritone Johann Vogl singing, but also frequently improvise waltzes and dances at the piano – waltzes and dances that he would then carefully write down after the event.

This period, from 1814 to 1817, was a hugely prolific one, even for Schubert, a composer who would soon become known not just for the quality but also the quantity of his output. More importantly, 1816 saw the arrival of his first commissioned work, a cantata called *Prometheus*, for which he was paid the princely sum of 40 gulden. Although it was well received at the time, the score was lost in Schubert's own lifetime, so succeeding generations have had to take it on trust that it was a masterpiece.

The Schubertiads continued to prosper and were never short of music. Schubert's friend Vogl, who was very much in the autumn of his career as an opera singer, decided to devote himself to popularising the songs of his new-found musical comrade. Another of the Schubertiad group was a law student and amateur poet called Franz von Schober. Although not the most highly-regarded poet at the time or even now, there was one poem which he wrote that inspired Schubert to great musical heights.

An die Musik was written in 1817, a profoundly-felt testament to Schubert's own art. `recommended 2`

That same year, Schubert, still just 20, made a bold move. He decided to give up teaching in order to concentrate on composition, moving in with Schober's mother. But by late 1817, Schubert was *back* in teaching, due to changed family circumstances. The drudgery of teaching, as he saw it, was especially hard after his taste, not just of freedom but also of some early success. He temporarily switched to teaching the children of Count Esterházy, at Zseliz in Hungary, but, despite the prestige of the job, he could not bear it. He soon returned to his beloved Vienna.

Back home, Schubert was engaged on a number of small concert tours with Vogl, and they soon became a familiar fixture in the Viennese social scene. In the summer of 1819, they spent three months in a small town called Steyr, some 90 miles from Vienna, and the *"inconceivably lovely"* countryside, as Schubert put it, soon moved him to compose. The result was one of the most famous quintets in music, *The Trout.* `recommended 3`

Schubert was still just 22, and his prolific pace of composition continued. He wrote two operas in 1820, although neither was particularly popular. In fact, despite him being considered more or less the king of Lieder, he proved to be more of a court jester when it came to opera, with none of his works for the opera house ever achieving real success.

Schubert's social standing was unaffected, though, and his now legendary daytime routine became firmly entrenched. Almost without fail, he would compose in the morning, meet friends at coffee houses in the afternoon, and perform – usually at Schubertiads – in the evening. More importantly, perhaps, he also began to earn a lot more money from publication of his music. Up until now, being merely a composer and not a combined "composer/performer" – or singer/songwriter as we might say today – had deterred many publishers from accepting Schubert's work. He often had to rely on friends to organise subscription publication – a very common practice at the time – in which money was pooled from well-wishers to cover the costs of publication. His song, *Erlkönig*, for example, was published in this way and it earned him 32 ducats. `recommended 4`

The year 1822 saw the arrival of a work which stands almost alone in the Schubert repertoire – Symphony No. 8, the Unfinished. It brought him no money to speak of and stands on its own now, mainly because of its incompleteness – something which, when you look at the way Schubert worked, is remarkable. Schubert was a man of routine, as we know from his working day. He didn't like to move on to a new piece until the previous one was finished. So why didn't he finish the eighth symphony? It's not as if he didn't write any more symphonies – he was dotting the i's and crossing the t's on the ninth symphony by 1828. The most plausible theory appears to be that it simply held bad memories for him. Schubert had contracted syphilis in the same year that he'd composed the existing two movements of the eighth symphony, and many believe he simply didn't want to revisit it. Nevertheless, finished or not, it has become a staple of the repertoire. `recommended 5`

By 1823, Schubert was still just 26, and yet tragically in the autumn of his years. In the 1820s, if you contracted syphilis then it was almost certainly there to stay, as there was no known cure. Schubert would be ill from this point until his death, and this greatly contributed to the dearth of compositions from here on. It also meant that Schubert moved out of his friend Schober's house and back in with his family.

In 1824, in need of money, Schubert once again agreed to be music master to the Esterházy family, but this time only for a period of months. Regardless of the short stay, he longed for Vienna. *"I sit here, in the depths of the Hungarian countryside,"* he said, *"whither I unfortunately let myself be enticed a second time, without having a single person with whom I could speak a sensible word."*

By 1825, Schubert's reputation was probably reaching its peak. He was getting more and more work published, and three different firms were vying for his latest music. In fact, Schubert must have felt he had made it when he entered negotiations with one of the most famous publishers of all, at the time – namely, Artaria.

In 1826, Schubert was 29. He applied, very much with money in mind, for the post of vice-director of the Imperial Court Chapel, and was disappointed when he failed to secure it. Nevertheless, the Schubertiads continued, unabated, and it is said that Schubert spent much of 1826 *"seeing in the chimes"* of midnight in taverns and coffee houses. A year later,

COMPOSERS' NOTES NOTE

Our Lady of the Lake

In 1825, Schubert wrote a number of songs using Scott's *The Lady of the Lake*. One of them was known in its original German as *Ellen's Gesang III*. Later, Latin words were substituted for the German and it is in this guise that it is most familiar today – *Ave Maria*. recommended **6**

on 19 March 1827, Schubert visited Beethoven on his deathbed. The two had lived in the same city for years but, up until this point, had never met. One week later, Beethoven died and was buried in the Wahring cemetery. Schubert was one of the 36 torch bearers in the funeral procession.

By 1828, Schubert was feverish and unwell. He managed, however, to put the finishing touches to the great C major Symphony, which was completed by March. The *Winterreise* song cycle was also performed in this year, in both Munich and Berlin, but to a lukewarm reception. recommended **7** He received 30 gulden for some small impromptus and a five-part chorus, as well 60 gulden for a trio. These rather small sums which

Schubert was receiving show how precarious his finances were, even in his final year. He also couldn't afford a holiday, despite the fact that his health might have benefited.

Schubert moved in with a friend the same year, in the then largely rural suburb of Neue Wieden, and it was hoped that the country atmosphere might prove beneficial for his health. However, the house was damp and fairly unclean and, ironically, it's thought it might even have hastened the end. While working on corrections to the proofs of *Winterreise* on 19 November 1828, at 3pm, he died.

After his death, his personal effects were assessed at 63 gulden. Funeral expenses and money needed to pay his medical bills came to 1,000 gulden, all of which had to be paid for by posthumous publication fees.

RECOMMENDED LISTENING

 GRETCHEN AM SPINNRADE
Barbara Bonney/Geoffrey Parsons

 AN DIE MUSIK
Dietrich Fischer-Diskau/Gerald Moore

 THE TROUT
Bryn Terfl/Malcolm Martineau (song version)
Brendel/Riegelbauer/Duven/Zimmermann/
Zehetmair (quintet version)

 ERLKÖNIG
Dietrich Fischer-Dieskau/Gerald Moore

 **"UNFINISHED" SYMPHONY NO. 8**
New York Philharmonic Orchestra/Leonard
Bernstein

 AVE MARIA
Angela Gheorghiu/Romanian National Chamber
Choir

 WINTERREISE
Matthias Goerne/Alfred Brendel

HANDEL'S NOTES

Name: Georg Friedrich Händel
(later George Frideric Handel)

Nationality: German

Born: 23 February 1685
That's the same year that ... John Bunyan wrote part 2 of The Pilgrim's Progress

Died: 14 April 1759
The same year that ... William Wilberforce was born

Wealth rating: £££

Georg Friedrich Händel was born in the northern German town of Halle in 1685 – the same year that J.S. Bach was born. He was the son of a barber-surgeon. Despite Handel's early gift for music, his father expected that his son would either take up the family firm or go into the field of law. Handel resisted, and a battle ensued. All music was thus banned in the house, and it is said that Handel had to smuggle a small keyboard into the house when his father was away, and he would sneak up into the attic to play it. In the end, his father relented and the eight-year-old boy was given music lessons until he was 11. At this point, his teacher, Friedrich Zachow, declared that there was nothing else he could teach little Georg. Interestingly, there is no record of any further music lessons for Handel beyond this point.

At 17 years of age, Handel was appointed organist at the Domkirche in Halle with a salary of 50 thaler a year and free lodgings. For this he had to play on *"Sundays, thanksgivings and feast days"* and look after the organ, supervising any repairs. When he was 18, he moved to Hamburg with a view to taking on pupils or playing in the opera orchestra to pay his way. It seems he must have achieved this: his mum sent him a letter with money in it, only to find him, some months later, returning the money and including some extra for her and the family.

By 1706, despite sending regular money home, he managed to save 200 ducats from his work, and so set off for fame and more fortune on a tour of Italy. His first opera, *Rodrigo*, earned him the princely sum of 100 sequins and a dinner service. When he got back from Italy, his fame had returned ahead of him and, in 1710 at the age of just 25 years, he accepted the job of Kapellmeister to the elector of Hanover, on a salary of 1,000 thaler. Handel was obviously well aware of his worth because he negotiated some very favourable terms which allowed him to travel for up to 12 months at a time and still retain his job.

With his new contract as well as letters of introduction in his bag, Handel journeyed to London, where he was an immediate hit. The England of Queen Anne had just three or four royal composers and Handel's timing could not have been better. Jeremiah Clarke, the main royal composer, had just taken his own life, and John Blow, his deputy, had also died. The composers remaining were Croft and Eccles. Not exactly household names: Handel saw them off, as it were, and immediately became the royal favourite.

It was at this point, in 1711, that Handel wrote his opera *Rinaldo*. It was a huge success and made Handel so much money that he was able to invest £500 into the infamous South Sea Company. Luckily for Handel, he withdrew his investment long before the bubble burst. In fact, Handel was doing so well that he had neglected to return to his position in Hanover, as Kapellmeister to the elector. Yet here comes one of those amazing turns of events which you simply couldn't make up. The reigning monarch, Queen Anne, died. In her place, who was made king of England? It was none other than the elector of Hanover – Handel's employer – who became George I. Once Handel had overcome his embarrassment at having been absent from his job in Hanover for two years, he was immediately employed on a pension of £400 per year, plus a further £200 per year from the Princess of Wales. As is now well documented, it was for George I that Handel came up with his *Water Music*. The problems of getting 50 oboes, bassoons, horns, trumpets, strings, flutes and recorders playing in a barge on the Thames is not a job to be envied and yet, somehow, Handel and his team pulled it off. The bill for the musicians alone, for that one night, was £150. George I loved it. **recommended 1**

By this point, Handel had lost his umlaut. That is to say, he had become a British citizen and changed his name from Georg Friedrich Händel to George Frideric Handel: a subtle yet important difference, no doubt.

In 1719, with society now firmly hooked on Italian opera, the Royal Academy of Music was set up to promote and profit from the latest musical craze. It was run by the successful theatre impresario, John Jacob Heidegger, and Handel was called upon to source singers and players for the new venture. It was a subscription affair, with around 60 or so investors all paying in the region of £200 each, as well as the king himself supplying a yearly bounty of £1,000. In all, the total subscription came to around £16,000, some indication of how hot a property opera was at the time.

During the next few years, Italian opera became the biggest money-making venture of the entire music scene. After four seasons, Handel was comfortably able to afford to move into a new house in London's Brooke Street. The house is still there, as a Handel museum, sharing its musical honours with a later resident, the guitarist Jimi Hendrix.

In 1727, the general euphoria in the music world was momentarily silenced when King George died on a trip to Hanover. When the Prince of Wales was proclaimed George II on 11 October, Handel supplied four coronation anthems for the service: *Let thy Hand be Strengthened, My Heart is Inditing, The King shall Rejoice* and, of course, the one which has been sung at virtually every coronation since, *Zadok the Priest.* (recommended **2**)

The year 1728 dawned and the public's desire for Italian opera was on the wane. Opera sung in English was having a rebirth, fuelled in part by the success of John Gay's *The Beggar's Opera.* Handel refused to pull his money out of Italian opera and, over the next few seasons, lost more and more of his own amassed fortune. Some estimates put his personal losses at around £10,000. It is even thought that it was beginning to have an effect on the composer's health too. He sated the appetite of his debtors with high-profile, high-earning concerts where he would play organ concertos and premiere new anthems. He still dabbled in his beloved Italian opera, though, even coming up with the odd hit, such as the one from his 1738 offering, *Xerxes*, premiered at the Kings Theatre, Haymarket on 15 April that year. One of the arias, despite being marked "Larghetto" has now become known, oddly enough, as Handel's Largo – or "Ombra mai fu". (recommended **3**)

Despite his lack of good fortune, Handel stayed on in London, partly licking his wounds and partly wondering what the next big thing might be. It was around the same time that Dublin was proving to be a minor magnet to composers who visited London. It was proving to be a small but significant satellite market, and it became increasingly common that, if you were "doing London" – as many composer/performers were – you would "do Dublin", too. That is, you would include it on your concert tour. On 21 November 1741, the Dublin Gazette announced that "*last Wednesday, the celebrated Dr Handell*" – with 2 Ls! – "*arrived here in the packet boat from Holyhead*". He had planned to be there just a short while, but a rapturous reception persuaded him to extend his stay. In the end, he spent a full nine months in Dublin and grew to trust the local musicians and singers much more than he thought he would. He was persuaded to premiere his latest work there: an oratorio that he'd been composing over the last four months, and planning to unveil in London. The premiere of *Messiah* was a huge success – a hall built for 400 had to accommodate 700 on the night. Its popularity was predicted – ladies were asked to come *"without hoops"*, that is, without their wide-hooped dresses – so there would be more room. Gents were asked to attend without swords, for the same reason. The sum collected on the door that night was £400, of which £127 went to charities: a staggering success. **recommended 4**

Messiah did as much to rejuvenate Handel's spirits as it did his fortunes. As soon as he was back in London, he was signed up to compose a Lenten series of oratorios, sponsored by the Prince of Wales. They were to be mounted – unstaged – in Covent Garden, through the end of the winter and beginning of spring 1743. The season opened with *Samson*, the tale of the blinding of the mighty strongman, adapted from Milton's poem. Not only

COMPOSERS' NOTES NOTE

Musical jeanius

The "Sarabande" from Handel's Suite No. 11 in D minor languished in obscurity until a few years ago. It probably earned Handel nothing in his lifetime, being a mere bi-product of his annual salary. The question is: if he could have had royalties from its rebirth as the soundtrack to a very trendy TV ad for Levi jeans, how much would Handel's "Sarabande" have earned him then? **recommended 5**

was the whole season a risk for Handel – he was now effectively backing oratorio as "the next big thing" against the still-popular English opera – but *Samson* itself was a bit of a gamble. At a time when castrati were still the most highly prized and paid voices of their age, Handel wrote the part of Samson for tenor solo – the first major role for a tenor written outside France. *Samson* became a big hit for Handel, and was performed eight times in the first season. **recommended** *6* At the time of writing it, Handel was in the early stages of going blind himself, and it is said that years later, when totally blind, he could not listen to the aria "Total Eclipse" from *Samson* without being moved to tears.

Handel's fortunes – and his health – continued to go both up and down in the years following *Samson*. He championed Italian operas once again at the Haymarket theatre, but was unsuccessful. A series of four further oratorios was cancelled after the first one, much to the annoyance of its subscribers. In 1746, though, a good run with his oratorio *Judas Maccabaeus* allowed him to bank £600. This was followed by a performance of his oratorio *Joshua*, which netted him another £250.

In 1748, the peace of Aix-la-Chapelle ended the War of the Austrian Succession, and "the powers that be" commissioned a grand firework display in London's Green Park, to celebrate. The wooden structure on which the fireworks were to be set was 410-feet long by 114-feet high, built in a classical style with colonnades and a triumphal central arch. As part of his existing annuity, Handel was commissioned to write music for the event and – somewhat reluctantly, it seems – he set about composing a suite for 24 oboes, 12 bassoons, three pairs of timpani drums – in fact, the full works. After all, it would have to be heard above the noise of a firework display. A crowd of 12,000 people thronged into Green Park, and streets were jammed for hours before and after the event. The whole spectacle ended when the display caused the 400-foot wooden structure to catch fire, and the evening ended in an even-more-spectacular-than-intended 400-foot bonfire, razing the framework to the ground. It's said that the designer was so outraged that he set about the fireworks co-ordinator with his sword. Thankfully, Handel's music – the *Music for the Royal Fireworks* – survived. **recommended** *7*

That's more or less it for Handel. The final tally certainly suggests that he had far more ups than downs. Proceeds from his late oratorio, *Solomon* **recommended** *8*, swelled his bank-balance to around £8,000 within the year. Five days before he died in 1759, he added a codicil to his will, bequeathing £1,000 to the Society for Decayed Musicians and their families, as well as other smaller bequests to friends and acquaintances. In total, he left an estate of around £20,000. Quite an impressive figure.

RECOMMENDED LISTENING

 ### *WATER MUSIC*
The English Baroque Soloists/Sir John Eliot Gardiner

 ### *ZADOK THE PRIEST*
Choir of King's College, Cambridge/Academy of Ancient Music/Stephen Cleobury

 ### "OMBRA MAI FU" FROM *XERXES*
Andreas Scholl/Orchestra of the Age of Enlightenment/Sir Roger Norrington

 ### *MESSIAH*
Gabrielli Consort and Players/Paul McCreesh

 ### "SARABANDE" FROM SUITE NO. 11 IN D MINOR
City of Prague Philharmonic Orchestra/Paul Bateman

 ### "LET THE BRIGHT SERAPHIM" FROM *SAMSON*
Lynne Dawson/Orchestra of Harmony and Invention/Harry Christophers

 ### *MUSIC FOR THE ROYAL FIREWORKS*
English Concert/Trevor Pinnock

 ### "ARRIVAL OF THE QUEEN OF SHEBA" FROM *SOLOMON*
The Academy of Ancient Music/Christopher Hogwood

MASSENET'S NOTES

Name: Jules Émile Frédéric Massenet

Nationality: French

Born: 12 May 1842
That's the same year that ... Grace Darling died

Died: 13 August 1912
The same year that .. the Titanic sank

Wealth rating: 𝄢𝄢𝄢𝄢𝄢

Jules Émile Frédéric Massenet was born into a financially comfortable family in Montaud, near St Etienne, on 12 May 1842. His father was the boss of an engineering company which made agricultural tools. Massenet was taught music from an early age by his mother, a piano teacher. When he was five, Massenet's father retired from business and moved the family to Paris where Massenet's mother enlarged her teaching practice. She even began composing on a small scale.

When he was ten years old, Massenet enrolled at the Paris Conservatoire to study piano, despite still being at school. From then on, until his 20th birthday, he studied music to the detriment of everything else, intent on pursuing a musical career as soon as he could. When Massenet was 13, he was said to have been very impressed on hearing the composer Hector Berlioz conduct his own *L'enfance du Christ*. At 17, he won a prize for his piano playing, followed by a prize for his counterpoint when he was 19. In 1861, he began studying composition with the French composer Ambroise Thomas, and supported himself both by giving piano lessons and by playing timpani in the pit orchestra at Paris's Théâtre Lyrique. This part-time job gave him not only the money he needed to survive, but also the opportunity to hear, first hand, the opera scores of Gounod and Gluck, as well as Mozart, Beethoven and Weber.

Massenet entered the French composers' competition, the Prix de Rome, when he was 20, but was unsuccessful. A year later, however, his cantata, *David Rizzio*, walked off with the Grand Prix. The prize gave Massenet an annual allowance of 3,000 francs for the next five years, as well as the customary two-year spell in Rome at the Villa Medici. The 3,000 francs then would be worth around £5,500 now. Out in Rome, Massenet travelled a great deal but composed only a little. He met Franz Liszt who introduced him to his future wife. When he arrived home in 1866, he had at least a requiem, some songs and a suite for orchestra under his belt.

Back in Paris, he supplemented his 3,000 francs a year with money from piano teaching. He also tried to get some songs and piano pieces published, something which led him to the door of the publisher Georges Hartmann. Hartmann became not only Massenet's publisher but also his mentor for some 20 years. Around the same time, he was commissioned to write an opera for the Opéra-Comique. The result, *La grand'-tante*, was premiered there on 3 April 1867. Massenet's 35 years as an opera composer had begun.

Between 1867 and 1870, Massenet competed to be a part of the Paris music scene, one that included the likes of Bizet, Saint-Saëns, Delibes, Fauré, and Lalo. He was friends with all these composers and yet often found himself vying for the same commissions. Early on, he began to doubt his ability as an opera composer, particularly after one reviewer declared to all Paris that Massenet was clearly an orchestral composer, and not destined to write for the theatre.

Maybe this is why he left his second opera, *Manfred*, unfinished, while his third, *Méduse*, was rather rudely interrupted by the siege of Paris in 1870. During the real-life drama that unfolded, Massenet – now 28 years old – served in the National Guard. After the war, he was reinvigorated. He had a number of successful operas, including the grand opera, *The King of Lahore*, one of the first to be heard at the brand new Opéra Garnier. When he was 36, he was appointed professor of composition at the conservatoire. This brought with it a salary of 3,000 francs a year – not a terrible wage, but nothing compared to the salary of the conservatoire director, Thomas, who was earning 10,000 francs – that's the equivalent of somewhere in the region of £19,000 today. The appointment, although welcome financially, appears to have ruined his relationship with Saint-Saëns, who was also in the running for the job. Massenet retained the job, however, for the next 18 years, earning a reputation as an expert and yet very human teacher.

Meanwhile, the success of *The King of Lahore* meant Massenet had been noticed not just at home but abroad. Ricordi, the most famous Italian music publisher, was particularly impressed and commissioned a new opera. Massenet soon settled down to a composing life of winters in Paris and summers in different country retreats, with the occasional visit to oversee a foreign premiere. The opera for Ricordi, *Hérodiade*, was premiered in Brussels in 1881 – objections to the biblical love story at its heart prevented it from having a Paris premiere. His next opera would have no such problems.

For this, Massenet got together with Offenbach's librettist, Henri Meilhac, and adapted the novel by the Abbé Prévost from 1731, *L'histoire du chevalier de grieux et de Manon Lescaut*. The composer Auber had already set it in 1854 – indeed, Puccini would set it again in 1893 – but Massenet's version, *Manon*, premiered at the Opéra-Comique in the January of 1884, confirmed him as the leading opera composer of his generation. The opera itself has never left the international repertoire, its popularity never waning. **recommended 2** and **recommended 3**

So, by 1884 Massenet was 42 years old, and his opera *Manon* had just premiered triumphantly at Paris's Opéra-Comique.

It was his biggest hit to date and opened the floodgates to a torrent of offers. Massenet was able to choose his librettists, his singers and even his theatres. Opera now began to account for the overwhelming majority of his output, while other areas of music – chiefly orchestral – declined to virtually nothing.

Ironically, Massenet's next opera, *Montalte*, flopped completely. He recycled much of the music into his subsequent opera, *Le cid*, which did rather better in 1885. The opera after *Le cid*, despite being a long time coming, would prove to be another great money-earner for Massenet.

He'd had an idea for an opera about Goethe's eponymous poet, Werther, four years before *Manon* but had never yet set pen to paper. Hartmann, his publisher and mentor, was keen to get him to work on the idea so he hired an 18th-century apartment in Versailles, and suggested that Massenet work there for a while – Hartmann was apparently well aware that Massenet worked best when stimulated according to the subject matter on which he was working. Hartmann also suggested a visit to Wetzlar to see where Goethe's original had been written. It appears that the apartment and the visit did the trick. By 1887, *Werther* was ready. **recommended 4**

So – just how much did the Paris Opéra-Comique pay Massenet, the new king of opera, for his new masterpiece? The answer is: precisely nothing. They looked at the score, prevaricated for a bit, and then decided it was too depressing. Despite "Massenet" being the name on every opera-goer's lips at the time, they rejected his new work. As luck would have it, Vienna staged *Manon* in 1890 and immediately wanted another Massenet opera to follow it. Massenet had *Werther* more or less in his back pocket – all done and dusted. It was premiered in February 1892 and, despite its bleak storyline, was soon a smash hit on the international stage. Paris then did a u-turn and, two years later, *Werther* was staged at the Opéra-Comique.

After *Werther*, Massenet continued his output of operas. *Esclarmonde* was written for the 1889 Paris Exposition. The huge "grand opera" *Le mage*, followed in 1891. But that same year, Massenet's publisher and friend Hartmann went bankrupt. Despite being unaffected, financially, by Hartmann's state of affairs – his catalogue was bought up by the publishers Heugel, and his financial arrangements were more or less unchanged – the composer was deeply affected, personally, by his friend's problems.

Massenet next looked to the work of the novelist Anatole France, in particular the story of a monk who sets out to convert a famous courtesan, only to end up falling for her charms. Massenet soon had the score – *Thaïs* – ready for the Opéra-Comique, with his favourite soprano Sybil Sanderson in the title role. Eventually, it opened at the newer, grander Opéra Garnier, with Sanderson causing a scandal by "accidentally" exposing her breast on the opening night – Janet Jackson wasn't the first and no doubt won't be the last. This opera had a heady mixture of religion and sex. In fact, when it played at the New Orleans opera house in 1973, it was the first time a soprano had sung totally nude. Despite the racy nature of the plot, it has always been on the fringes of the standard opera repertoire. On the fringes, that is save for one section, which has won a place in the music-loving public's heart ever since it was first heard. It is the music which is played for a humble change of scenery in Act 2. It is called "Méditation". recommended **5**

When Ambroise Thomas, the director of the conservatoire, died in 1896, Massenet was immediately offered the job, on a salary of more than 10,000 francs. He not only turned it down, but also took the opportunity to hand in his notice as a 3,000-francs-a-year professor of composition, citing lack of time as his reason. To be fair, with the pressures of his many operas and their international premieres, he felt he had too often had to send in a deputy to take his composition class. In addition, some reports estimate that Massenet was, by this time, earning around 150,000 francs a year from the publishing rights and royalties to his work. This is the equivalent of around £290,000 today.

Sapho was his next big hit, in 1897, followed by *Cendrillon* two years later. It was around this time that Massenet decided to buy his own chateau at Egreville, around 20 miles south of Fontainebleu, where he was able to spend the summers completing his operas. By this time, he was hardly out of the general repertoires of London, Milan, Vienna and Paris, as well as other opera capitals of the world.

His opera, *Griselidis*, was premiered at the Opéra-Comique in 1901, breaking box-office records with receipts in the region of 10,000 francs – around £19,000 today – while his next, *Le jongleur de Notre Dame*, opened in Monte Carlo. His piano concerto of 1903 flopped and has never been included in concert pianists' standard repertoire. Other operas from this late period include *Thérèse, Ariane, Don Quichotte* ◖recommended 6◗ and *Chérubin*, which is based on the later antics of Mozart's character, Cherubino, from *The Marriage of Figaro*. Despite the notion that he was running out of melodic ideas, Massenet never gave up writing operas. He also never gave up his own particular formula, unaffected by the trappings of newcomers like Debussy and Ravel. In the last five years of his life, he wrote five full-length operas. His income from these last few years alone was said to have been in the region of 700,000 francs alone, which, if true, would be the equivalent of around £1.3 million today.

Towards the end of his life, Massenet began a series of memoirs, published weekly in the journal *Echo de Paris* in which he reminisced about his life.

RECOMMENDED LISTENING

 ÉLÉGIE
Joshua Bell/Academy of St Martin-in-the-Fields/
Michael Stern

 "ADIEU, NOTRE PETITE TABLE" FROM
MANON
Leontyne Price/New Philharmonia Orchestra/
conductor?

 "JE SUIS SEUL!" FROM *MANON*
Marcelo Alvarez/Nice Opera Orchestra/Mark Elder

 "POURQUOI ME REVEILLER" FROM
WERTHER
Placido Domingo/Cologne Radio Symphony
Orchestra/Riccardo Chailly

 "MEDITATION" FROM *THAÏS*
Anne-Sophie Mutter/Vienna Philharmonic
Orchestra/James Levine

 SECOND INTERLUDE FROM *DON*
QUICHOTTE
National Opera Orchestra of Monte Carlo/Sir John
Eliot Gardiner

BEETHOVEN'S NOTES

Name: Ludwig van Beethoven

Nationality: German

Born: (probably) 16 December 1770
That's the same year that ... James Cook discovered Botany Bay

Died: 26 March 1827
The same year that ... the London Evening Standard *was first published*

Wealth rating: £ £

Ludwig van Beethoven was the eldest surviving son of a relatively well-off family in the small, provincial, but highly-cultural German city of Bonn. He was probably born on 16 December 1770: surprisingly, there is no record of his birth, but we do know he was baptised on the 17th and that usually happened the day after birth.

Beethoven's grandfather – who he adored, and after whom he was named – was Kapellmeister at the elector's court in Bonn, the most senior musical position in the city, and was also a fine bass singer. Beethoven's father was also employed at the court as a tenor, but he soon degenerated as he spent less and less time singing and more and more time drinking.

Beethoven was brought up in a musical but somewhat chaotic household. His grandfather died when Beethoven was just three, but the boy had inherited his grandfather's musical talent – and more. At the age of just 13, he was appointed assistant court organist in Bonn on a salary of just 100 thalers – but he was on his way.

Trouble loomed, though. Five years later, his father's voice was described, in an official report to the elector, as "stale", and he was forced to take early retirement. His salary was halved and paid to his eldest son for the upkeep of his brothers.

Beethoven was, in effect, now head of the family. The responsibility was the last thing he needed, given that his musical reputation was rising in leaps and bounds. When war against France brought chaos to Bonn and forced the elector to disband his court, Beethoven left Bonn and, with the help of his patron Count Waldstein, he made for Vienna to study with Haydn, intending to stay for a year or two. In the end, he never returned.

Beethoven was now a young man of 22, and newly arrived in Vienna – the capital city of music – with a salary promised from the elector back in Bonn. Given his meticulous book-keeping, you might think he was a man in control of his finances:

> *"Black silk stockings: 1 ducat*
> *1 pair of winter silk stockings: 1 florin 40 kreutzers*
> *Boots: 6 florins*
> *Shoes: 1 florin 30 kreutzers*

Well dressed, then.

And living expenses:

> *House rent: 14 florins*
> *Pianoforte: 6 florins 40 kreutzers*
> *Heating: each time, 12 kreutzers*
> *Meals, with wine* (of course)*: 16½ florins*
> *To the housekeeper no more than 7 florins, since the rooms*
> *are so close to the ground."*

And even:

> *"Chocolate for Haydn and me: 22 kreutzers.*
> *Coffee for Haydn and me: 6 kreutzers."*

That was probably the last time that Beethoven was ever so careful with his money. The promised salary from Bonn dried up, mainly due to the war and, in no time, Beethoven was earning a reputation of an altogether different kind: for dressing badly in ill-fitting clothes that often needed repair, and for never once splashing out to buy a wig to cover his tousled and chaotic hair.

In need of money, Beethoven took on piano pupils – something which he hated. With his heart not in the lessons, he was not exactly a demanding teacher. But he did fall in love with one of his pupils and refused to take money from her. Instead, and by way of an engagement present for her, he composed a new piano sonata. Her name was Giulietta Guicciardi and the name of her sonata was "Moonlight". **recommended 2**

Beethoven was fortunate with his patrons. There was Count Waldstein in Bonn. Then his greatest patron in his early years in Vienna was Prince Lichnowsky who, realising the young composer needed money, offered to pay Beethoven an annuity of 600 florins until he secured paid employment. Also, in April 1800, he held his first benefit concert in Vienna which, given the size of the hall – the daunting Burgtheater alongside the Imperial Palace – and the size of orchestra demanded by Beethoven, would not have earned him very much at all.

Three years after the benefit concert, he managed to earn a massive 1,800 florins from a similar affair at which he premiered two great works, his second symphony and third piano concerto. Only months later, he composed his greatest symphony to date – his No. 3, the "Eroica" – in the small village of Döbling, just south of Vienna. **recommended 3** He was now asking 90 florins – a substantial sum – from publishers for a new work, and was able to write to a friend: *"My compositions bring me in a good deal . . . People no longer come to an arrangement with me. I state my price and they pay."*

Maybe that's why, in a fit of temper, he smashed the marble bust of Prince Lichnowsky that the prince had given him, knowing it was likely to lead to the prince terminating his annuity: which he did.

Thankfully for Beethoven, the money kept coming in. He sold the English publishing rights for six new works to Clementi for £200, and the Viennese rights for the same works for 1,600 florins. The fourth symphony brought him 500 florins from the nobleman who commissioned it. Then, when the same count offered him a further 500 florins to compose another, Beethoven accepted and composed his now iconic fifth symphony. Think what he could have charged today.

Given all this money, you could be forgiven for thinking he was living in some style – but this was not the case. Beethoven wouldn't buy new clothes or furnish his apartment properly and his friends were frankly appalled at the conditions in which he lived. So where did his money go? Well, he ate out for practically every meal, he spent many evenings in the taverns, and his friends frequently commented on his generosity – he loaned money to his friends and his brothers.

In 1808 – one of several years that could be called an *annus horribilis* for Beethoven – he was promised a benefit concert that was postponed. Then postponed again. And again. As a result, when an emissary arrived from the court of King Jerome of Westphalia, offering him the post of Kapellmeister and inviting him to name his price, Beethoven demanded 600 ducats a year. It was immediately accepted.

This caused a furious panic among his friends. How could they allow Beethoven, with his increasing deafness and his overt

---

COMPOSERS' NOTES NOTE

Fake Für

"Für Elise" should actually be "Für Therese", because it was almost certainly composed for Therese Malfatti, a pupil with whom Beethoven had fallen in love. He presented the piece to her as an engagement present at a party in front of all her family and friends, then got so drunk he couldn't play it for her. In the end, when the work was found (after Therese's death), the publisher had difficulty reading Beethoven's virtually illegible scrawl on the front page. As a result it was published as "Für Elise".

recommended **4**

eccentricities, to go and live abroad? So his greatest patron of all, Archduke Rudolph, together with two aristocratic colleagues, promised Beethoven an annuity of 4,000 florins on the sole condition that he remain in Vienna. Beethoven agreed.

So, was this the financial security that Beethoven needed? Not before a last-minute hitch of gargantuan proportions. The Austrian government – bled dry by years of war against France – devalued the currency by a massive four-fifths. One of Beethoven's aristocratic backers soon went bankrupt and was forced to flee home to Bohemia. Another fell off his horse while hunting and was killed. However, Archduke Rudolph, in an extraordinary act of generosity, made up the difference. Perhaps this is one reason Beethoven dedicated more pieces of music to Archduke Rudolph than to any other single person. One such work is the "Emperor", the last piano concerto Beethoven composed, although he was only 38. ◖recommended **5**◗ Beethoven's hearing was already deteriorating so badly, he knew he could no longer perform his own concertos in public.

Despite the annuity, Beethoven still complained of poverty. He wrote to a friend: *"I have just lost 600 gulden a year from my salary . . . and had to face hardship for several years as well as a complete loss of my salary . . . My poor unfortunate brother has just died . . . I must have given him 10,000 gulden."*

And a year later he says: *"My income amounts to 3,400 gulden in paper money. I pay 1,100 for rent, and my servant and his wife cost me about 900 gulden. Moreover I have to support my little nephew entirely."*

That last comment concerning his nephew can only be described as entirely Beethoven's own fault. He had taken his sister-in-law to court in order to gain custody of *her* son, his nephew. It was a long, drawn-out affair, which sapped him creatively. Ultimately, Beethoven won the case, but not before having lined numerous lawyers' pockets with his money.

By 1820, he was in debt to his publishers. This may explain why he was quite happy to sell a new work *exclusively* to one publisher and then blithely sell it again to another, something which brought the threat of legal action down on his head. In fact, Beethoven's final years were dominated by money problems. The Philharmonic Society of London (now the Royal Philharmonic Society) alleviated them slightly by offering him £50 for a new symphony, and then sending him a gift of £100 when they heard he was seriously ill. They very much backed a winner in this respect – the symphony which Beethoven would write for them was his Symphony No. 9, the "Choral". **recommended 6**

The ninth symphony was Beethoven's crowning glory, one of the most loved pieces of music ever composed – although the benefit concert at which it was first performed earned him very little money. Upon his death, on 26 March 1827, Beethoven's total estate was valued at 9,885 florins and 13 kreutzer: that's less than £1,000. During his life, it is fair to say he earned a small fortune but, for one reason or another – mostly down to his carelessness with money – it slipped through his fingers.

RECOMMENDED LISTENING

 CANTATA ON THE DEATH OF EMPEROR JOSEPH II
Janice Watson/Jean Rigby/John Mark Ainsley/José van Dam/Corydon Singers/Corydon Orchestra/ Matthew Best

 "MOONLIGHT" SONATA *(The "Moonlight" Sonata's real title is actually* Sonata quasi una fantasia *– sonata in the style of a fantasia. That's how Beethoven – and Giulietta – knew it. The "Moonlight" label came thanks to a German music critic who compared it to the moon setting over Lake Lucerne.)*
Wilhelm Kempff

"EROICA" SYMPHONY
Tonhalle Orchestra Zurich/David Zinman

 FÜR ELISE
Balázs Szokolay

"EMPEROR" PIANO CONCERTO
Maurizio Pollini/Berlin Philharmonic Orchestra/
Claudio Abbado

SYMPHONY NO. 9 ("CHORAL")
Tonhalle Orchestra Zurich/Swiss Chamber Choir/
David Zinman

MENDELSSOHN'S NOTES

Name:	Jakob Ludwig Felix Mendelssohn-Bartholdy
Nationality:	German
Born:	3 February 1809

That's the same year that ... the "Two Thousand Guineas" was established at Newmarket

Died:	4 November 1847

The same year that ... Emily Brontë wrote Jane Eyre

Wealth rating:	💷💷💷💷

Jakob Ludwig Felix Mendelssohn-Bartholdy was born on 3 February 1809 in Hamburg and I think it's fair to say that, of all the composers in this book, Mendelssohn was the one born into by far the wealthiest background. His grandfather was the celebrated thinker Moses Mendelssohn, who was responsible for shaping much of 18th-century enlightenment philosophy and literature. His father, Abraham, was an influential Jewish banker who, along with Mendelssohn's uncle, Joseph, owned and ran a powerful Hamburg bank.

When Felix was six years old, his father had him baptised into the Christian faith, following suit himself a few years later – partly because of his enlightenment beliefs and partly because, pragmatically, he knew how many doors were closed to Jews, particularly in the world of music. By this time, Mendelssohn had only received piano lessons from his mother but, when he was ten, his father paid for expensive lessons with Ludwig Berger, a much-admired teacher of the time. He also funded theory and violin lessons with money clearly being no object. Between the ages of 11 and 21, Mendelssohn also visited Goethe, with whom he built up an invaluable artistic relationship.

One invaluable asset that Mendelssohn's father's money also bought him was experience. When he was 16, his father bought a house at No. 3, Leipziger Strasse, Berlin, and the house soon became a focal point for culture in the city. The Sunday-night concerts were attended by "the great and the good" of the day – among the regular guests were the philosopher Hegel, the music critic Adolf Marx, as well as leading actors, theologians and writers. It was in this year, against this background and inspired by the classical poetry of his mentor Goethe, that Mendelssohn came up with his first truly mature work – his Octet. **recommended 1**

By 1829, and still only 20 years old, Mendelssohn already had a number of mature compositions under his belt. All who heard him play proclaimed him the second Mozart. But it's to neither his own music, nor Mozart's, for that matter, that Mendelssohn turned next. Instead, he decided almost single-handedly to revive the flagging reputation of one of the greatest baroque composers – J.S. Bach.

Mendelssohn had become familiar with Bach while at the Berlin Singakademie, where his music was used as much for teaching as for its art. In the concert halls of Germany, Bach was unheard – his oratorios and passions were considered too unwieldy, too large-scale – in fact, simply too unfashionable to put on. Mendelssohn decided to stage a performance of the *St Matthew Passion*, a concert which proved to be a resounding success and triggered the modern revival of the previously forgotten Bach.

That same year, Mendelssohn decided to travel. Being rather comfortably off for money meant he had already seen quite a bit of the world, having visited, among other places, Italy, Switzerland, France and Silesia. In 1829, at the insistence of his parents, Mendelssohn embarked on a full six years of travelling, setting off first for England. Here, he was hailed as a bit of a celebrity. He conducted the premiere of his C minor symphony and, as is now well known, visited Scotland. It was here, on Staffa, that he found inspiration for perhaps his most famous piece.

On 8 August 1829, Mendelssohn was staying in Oban but decided to make a day trip to Fingal's Cave, where he jotted down the opening bars of an overture. His travelling companion, Karl Klinhemann, wrote that day in his diary that Mendelssohn *"is on better terms with the sea as a musician than he is as an individual or a stomach!"*

The composer, for his part, also wrote later: *"How much has happened between my last letter and this! The most fearful sickness, Staffa, scenery . . ."*

Nevertheless, Mendelssohn seems to have taken away happy memories of the time, although it was a good few years before he gave the resulting work he had written here the title *Fingal's Cave* or the *Hebrides Overture.* **recommended 2**

COMPOSERS' NOTES NOTE

Welcome to Britain

Leafing through Mendelssohn's diary from his 1829 British visit reveals some rather interesting notes. Conwy, in Wales, for example, is commemorated with just the single-line note on 26 August: *"I arrived perhaps wetter than I'd ever been in my entire life!"* while an entry from his journey back from Scotland includes things that only a musician would note: *"Through the fog, we see lamps gleaming along the horizon, the smoke from factories envelops us on all sides . . . [and] . . . one coach horn blows in B flat, another in D!"*

Mendelssohn was introduced to the British public at four large-scale concerts, which more or less sealed his name as one of the greatest living composers. He also found time to fit in a trip to Rhydymwyn, to visit important business contacts of his father's, the Taylors, on the estate of Coed-Du, now a hospital.

Back home, Mendelssohn's reputation grew ever greater. Still only 21, he was offered the chair of music at Berlin University but turned it down. He continued his travels through Florence, Rome, Naples, Pompei, Paris and then London again. Then in 1833, the year of his "Italian" Symphony **recommended 3**, Mendelssohn accepted the post of city music director in Düsseldorf, on an annual salary of 600 thaler, with three months leave per year. During his stay in Düsseldorf, he spent a lot of his time trying to do for Handel what he had done for Bach, devoting some of his obligatory eight concerts a year to raising Handel's profile.

Though disagreements led to him leaving the job after only a year, he soon found alternative employment – as conductor of the famous Leipzig Gewandhaus Orchestra. The salary was better, too. The terms for his tenure were negotiated for Mendelssohn by his lawyer, Konrad Schleinitz, and they amounted to 1,000 thaler and a whopping six months off per year. I'd say the lawyer earned his fee on that occasion.

Over the next five years, Mendelsshohn's meticulous and passionate approach to conducting and music in general transformed the Leipzig orchestra into probably the best in the world. He championed not only composers like Mozart, Beethoven and Weber, but also performers too: during his stay, Clara Schumann gave 21 performances, and artists such as Liszt, Rubinstein, Vieuxtemps, the Swedish soprano Jenny Lind and the 13-year-old violin prodigy, Joseph Joachim all performed with Mendelssohn and the Gewandhaus orchestra.

In 1841, Friedrich Wilhelm the Third of Prussia died, and was succeeded by his son, Friedrich Wilhelm the Fourth. Friedrich the Fourth's new broom, as it were, clearly extended to music, and he decided to create a brand new Academy of the Arts. Friedrich wanted Mendelssohn as his Number 1 and so he was drafted in at a salary of 3,000 thaler per year and a brief to reform the Berlin music scene. In addition, he could keep his Gewandhaus position, so that meant that, at this point, he was on a staggering 4,000 thaler per year.

Mendelssohn's idea of reform was not the same as that of Friedrich the Fourth, and so Mendelssohn more or less left the post after a year or so. He was given a nominal title, in order that all parties saved face, and he was free once again to concentrate solely on Leipzig: not just the Gewandhaus, but also on a brand new project.

A prominent Leipzig lawyer had bequeathed around 20,000 thaler to the city to found *"a new institute for the arts"*. Clearly, Mendelssohn was the obvious choice to head it up and, when it opened in 1843, he had succeeded in attracting some huge names to its staff – Robert Schumann taught piano, the then legendary Ferdinand David taught violin and, later on, Clara Schumann and the Danish composer Neils Gade joined the team.

Just one year later, in a brief few weeks of holiday in the town of Soden, near Frankfurt, Mendelssohn found time in his now punishing schedule to compose – for his own pleasure and to no commission – his violin concerto. With Ferdinand David as soloist, it was premiered at the Leipzig Gewandhaus in 1845.
`recommended 4`

The two years following the violin concerto were to prove frantic ones for Mendelssohn. He seemed to be trying to fit as much in as he could, including, incidentally, a trip to Birmingham to conduct his new oratorio, *Elijah*. Principally, though, he kept up a furious schedule of concerts in Leipzig. At one concert, Mendelssohn conducted Schumann's piano concerto with Clara Schumann as soloist and Robert Schumann in the audience.

On 12 May 1847 in Frankfurt, Mendelssohn was greeted with the news that his beloved sister, Fanny, was dead. Hearing the news, he became unconscious, rupturing a blood vessel in his brain, something from which he never truly recovered. In Leipzig, to start the new concert season that year, his friends noticed that his appearance and general demeanour had changed. He died on 4 November 1847 before being able to conduct a single concert in the new season. He was only 38.

And that's Mendelssohn tallied. With a very prosperous family in his early years and a financially successful career to boot, Mendelssohn is one of the most solvent composers in this book.

RECOMMENDED LISTENING

 ### OCTET
Medici String Quartet/Alberni String Quartet

 ### *HEBRIDES OVERTURE*
Orchestra of the Champs-Elysées/Philippe Herreweghe

 ### "ITALIAN" SYMPHONY
Ulster Orchestra/Dmitri Sitkovetsky

 ### VIOLIN CONCERTO
Kyung-Wha Chung/Montreal Symphony Orchestra/Charles Dutoit

 ### SUITE FROM *A MIDSUMMER NIGHT'S DREAM*
Atlanta Symphony Orchestra/Yoel Levi

OFFENBACH'S NOTES

Name: Jacques Offenbach (Jacob Eberst)

Nationality: German (later became a French citizen)

Born: 20 June 1819
That's the same year that ... Keats wrote Hyperion

Died: 5 October 1880
The same year that ... Rodin sculpted The Thinker

Wealth rating: 🏛️🏛️🏛️🏛️

Jacques Offenbach was born Jacob Eberst on 20 June 1819 in Cologne. His father was a music teacher and bookbinder who had left his native town of Offenbach some 20 years earlier. As a result, his father was often known as "Der Offenbacher" – the man from Offenbach – or sometimes just simply Offenbach. Jacob was the seventh of Eberst's ten children, and from an early age he learnt to play violin and cello. Eventually, alongside his brother and sister, he formed a family piano trio and they played in the bars of Cologne to earn money. They also studied music with various Cologne teachers before being taken off to Paris by their father. Offenbach's father, by now a synagogue cantor, appears to have spotted the musical potential in his son and was desperate for him to receive better tuition. Jacob enrolled at the Paris Conservatoire and it was here that he started to become known as "Jacques". He also found a position with a synagogue choir.

By 1833, the 14-year-old composer was no longer Jacob Eberst but was instead known as Jacques Offenbach. He spent a year studying at the conservatoire before leaving and trying to gain a position playing cello in an orchestra. After a short time playing with two minor orchestras, he landed a job in the pit at the Opéra-Comique. This appears to have been a formative time for Offenbach: not only was he getting a good grounding in the operas that were playing every night at the Opéra-Comique, but he also managed to get himself some composition lessons from the well-known French opera writer, Fromental Halévy. The ensuing friendship with Halévy's son, Ludovic, would prove significant when he later came to search for a librettist.

Offenbach left the job at the Opéra-Comique when he was 19 and it was around this time that he struck up a friendship with the composer Friedrich von Flotow, who was just beginning to gain a name as an opera composer, but had yet to have his big hit with *Martha*. Flotow introduced Offenbach into the Parisian "salon" circle which would prove not only a crucial musical influence but also the catalyst for useful commissions. In addition, Offenbach found the Paris salons abundant in music pupils, another useful source of extra money. Offenbach and Flotow even joined forces – on cello and piano – to perform their own pieces in the well-to-do drawing rooms of Paris. As a result of this concerted PR push, at the age of 20, Offenbach gained his first commission – for a vaudeville piece called *Pascal et Chambord*.

It's interesting to see that, so far in Offenbach's life, the cello had been his main source of income, something which would be true for a few years yet. He appeared as a cellist with Rubinstein accompanying in 1841, then teamed up with Liszt for a cello and piano concert in his native Cologne two years later; a few years on, aged 25, he visited London and took part in concerts organised by the Musicians' Union which also included Mendelssohn and the violinist Joachim on the bill; he also took part in a royal musical celebration of Ascot Week at Windsor Castle. All this time, he was writing his music, principally opera and operetta, although his attempts to get his works performed often came to nothing. By this point, he was married – surely it was only a coincidence that his wife, Herminie, was related to a successful concert-booking agent.

The Opéra-Comique – despite his fledgling relationship with them – was unresponsive to Offenbach's entreaties for performances, and so he switched his allegiances to the Opéra National de Paris, run by the composer Adolph Adam, composer of, among other things, the Christmas carol *O Holy Night*. He approached the Opéra National when he was 29 – that was in the year 1848, the year of revolution. The machinations of 1848 meant his Opéra National hopes, too, came to nothing and he temporarily returned to Cologne.

Two years later, Offenbach's life was on an upward curve, with an appointment as conductor of the Comédie-Française. This gave him a valuable source of income, but only to play other people's music – he was still having no real success getting his own operas performed. In fact, by 1855 he was having such bad luck that he decided it was time to take a very bold step.

The year 1855 brought with it the Great Exhibition in Paris. Offenbach decided to rent his own small theatre for the whole exhibition season. It was called the Théâtre Marigny, and it was just off the Champs-Élysées. Offenbach quickly put together a small series of comic operas, and the whole thing launched as the Théâtre des Bouffes-Parisiens on 5 July that year.

It was a very brave move. Should it have failed, it could have resulted in total financial ruin. Offenbach's entrepreneurial risks paid off, though. His season was *the* musical success of the 1855 exhibition. All Paris seemed to be talking about it. He was soon able to hand in his notice as conductor of the Comédie-Française. Soon, he added to his summer season at the Marigny by hiring the Théâtre Comte for the winter season, and again experienced a huge success. In the summer of 1856, he was back once again in the Théâtre Marigny. From the following winter season on, he made the Théâtre Comte his permanent home. Success on this scale did not come cheap. The refurbishment of the Théâtre Comte as his permanent home cost him 80,000 French francs.

By 1857, Offenbach's success had prompted his wife's relative, the London musical agent John Mitchell, to bring the composer to the English capital. Not just Offenbach, but the entire company was transported from Paris to London, including Jacques' violin-playing brother Jules – with whom he used to play trios – who was now leader of the Bouffes-Parisiens. The two-month-long season ran from the beginning of May 1857 at the St James's Theatre.

Back in Paris a year later, Offenbach tasted his greatest success to date with his two-act operetta *Orphée aux enfers – Orpheus in the Underworld*. recommended **1** *Orpheus* was a financial as well as a musical *tour de force* and the 1859 receipts alone were a staggering 419,000 francs. In fact, its fantastic reception encouraged Offenbach to consider larger, fuller, grander operas as the way forward. *Le papillon* came in early 1860 and then the three-act *Barkouf* later the same year.

By now a naturalised Frenchman – and, indeed, already awarded a Legion d'Honneur – Offenbach resigned as director of the Bouffes-Parisiens in 1862, but still agreed to write extensively for the Marigny. He now had a family of seven, a house in the rue Lafite in Paris and a holiday home, the Villa Orphée, in the stylish Normandy resort of Étretat.

In order not only to make sure his fame spread, but also to combat pirated versions of his works, Offenbach now established himself in Vienna, too. In 1864, his opera *Die Rheinnixen* was premiered there, at the Hofoper, and Offenbach travelled to Vienna to oversee the performance. While there, he found time to compose some waltzes – his *Abendblätter* was his attempt to match Johann Strauss II's *Morgenblätter*, and it is often said that it was Offenbach's influence that started Strauss himself off on the road to operetta.

The same year saw another of his biggest successes – *La belle Hélène* recommended **2**, which was followed by *La vie parisienne* two years later. Even as early as *La vie parisienne*, though, Offenbach was realising that continued success in the opera world was becoming more and more expensive. His leading lady for *La vie parisienne* was costing him 4,500 francs a month. When you add up the costs of the entire cast, it was an expensive business.

By 1867 – Great Exhibition year again – Offenbach's music was being performed in three Paris theatres at the same time. In 1868 came the *huge* success that was *La périchole*. With *La périchole*, Offenbach managed to capture the zeitgeist of Paris in the late 19th century, as well as present some of his catchiest tunes in years. By its 50th performance, it had grossed receipts of 206,000 francs.

Through the war years of 1870 and 1871, Offenbach spent much of his time abroad, visiting Italy, London and Vienna. By the time he returned to Paris, opera tastes had begun to change. Ironically, the Parisian audiences' favourite appeared to be Lecocq, the composer who had first come to fame through a composition competition set up by Offenbach: the pupil was in the ascendant, the teacher appeared to be on the wane.

COMPOSERS' NOTES NOTE

Scents of humour

Offenbach was born in Cologne and it is said that he often used to sign himself with just his initial: *"O. de Cologne"*.

Offenbach's solution to the problem was, in 1873, to take over another theatre – the Théâtre de la Gaîté. This time, though, it would not just be for operas but also for plays. Initially, he had some success. The bizarrely named *King Carrot* had daily takings of 3,000 francs. He also staged huge, spectacular new versions of his old hits, like *Orpheus*. This, too, appeared to go well. Even though he was vastly expanding the operas – and the accompanying orchestra – he was still taking in huge amounts. The new *Orpheus* earned him a breathtaking 1.8 million francs. However, Offenbach wasn't the best businessman in the world, to say the least. An 1874 production of a Sardou play, *La haine*, was so badly managed, it forced the composer into bankruptcy.

Offenbach's financial life was now in crisis. In order to get back on track, he composed the music for a pantomime at London's Alhambra theatre. As odd as it might seem to us now – to have a composer like Offenbach working in panto in London – the result was *Whittington*, for which he was paid a much-needed 60,000 francs. He also accepted a concert tour of the USA, in time for the Philadelphia Centennial Exhibition of 1876, giving some 40 concerts, and conducting performances of his operettas *La vie parisienne* and *La jolie parfumeuse*. This punishing schedule of events and concerts appears to have done the trick. From then on, Offenbach was back on a successful footing, with minor triumphs even cropping up here and there, such as *Madame Favart* and *La fille de tambour-major*. Revivals of *Orpheus*, too, were always both popular and financially useful.

Chiefly, though, Offenbach spent most of his autumn years on *Les contes d'Hoffmann – The Tales of Hoffmann*. In 1880, he took some time off to go to Saint-Germain-en-Laye, to work on the score but, by September, his poor health forced him to return home to Paris. Offenbach had suffered gout for some time and it now appeared to be affecting his heart. He died in October the same year, the score of *The Tales of Hoffmann* still unfinished.

RECOMMENDED LISTENING

 ### *ORPHEUS IN THE UNDERWORLD*
English National Opera Orchestra and Chorus/ Mark Elder

 ### *LA BELLE HÉLÈNE*
Sadlers Wells Orchestra/John Matheson/ Alexander Faris

 ### *LES CONTES D'HOFFMAN*
Lyon Opera Orchestra and Chorus (soloists include Roberto Alagna and Sumi Jo)/Kent Nagano

PAGANINI'S NOTES

Name: Niccolò Paganini

Nationality: Italian

Born: 27 October 1782
That's the same year that ... the Montgolfier brothers invented the hot air balloon

Died: 27 May 1840
The same year that ... Nelson's Column was erected in Trafalgar Square

Wealth rating: £££££

Niccolò Paganini was born in Genoa on 27 October 1782. His family was by no means poor but, despite the fact that his father ran a successful shipping firm, Paganini's father didn't want his son to follow in his footsteps. As a child, he taught the young Niccolò violin and guitar, although his regime of practice appears to have verged on the barbaric. Food would be withheld if Paganini did not keep up a sufficient level of practice, and beatings were a regular occurrence. Before long – thankfully for Paganini – the father could teach the son no more, and the youngster was shipped off to a professional teacher. In turn, before much longer, this new teacher was equally at a loss as to how to advance Paganini's already phenomenal technique. The composer made his first public appearance playing the violin at the age of 11, but his father continued to fund not just violin lessons but also composition teaching.

It was during these early years that the young Paganini suffered an almost fatal attack of measles. In fact, so bad was it that his lifeless body was almost buried by mistake. Thankfully, he recovered, but it meant he would remain a sickly individual for the rest of his life.

When he was 16, important things began happening for Paganini. He made his first professional tour in Italy and began rather rapidly to make a name for himself. He also extricated himself from his father's rod of iron and set up on his own. With the newly-found independence came a newly-discovered penchant for women and money which would leave their mark on his life. It was around this time that he also composed the work that so inspired many other composers, the *24 Caprices*.
▭ recommended **1** and ▭ recommended **2**

At the age of 19, Paganini left his native Genoa for Lucca. His name had grown considerably in just three years, and he was able to command good fees. Offsetting this, he took to gambling and would often lose some six weeks of his concert earnings in just one night. Nevertheless, a full schedule of concert dates, possibly too many for such a sickly person, kept the cash flowing. Eventually, the gambling gained the upper hand, and on more than one occasion he was forced to pawn his violin in order to settle debts. Take one day, in Livorno. Paganini was due to play a concert that night, and yet all he had to play on was a pawn ticket. It's said that a benevolent local musician loaned him his valuable Guarnerius violin – in the violin world, a name almost as celebrated as Stadivarius. The following day, having been at the concert and heard what Paganini could do with his beloved, priceless violin, the local musician refused to accept it back and the composer kept it until the day he died.

By the turn of the 19th century, Paganini had become very famous indeed, albeit still only in his native Italy. He still had a bit of a problem with money which continued to show itself in an almost clinical desire to gamble. Could anything cure him of his addiction? Well, in the end, in a way, his violin cured him.

During one particularly bad night, Paganini came tantalisingly close to wagering his priceless Guarnerius violin to cover his evening's losses. He allegedly woke up the next morning, more than a little worse for wear, and thought about the night before. He soon realised how near he had been to losing the Guarnerius. Immediately, he vowed to give up gambling there and then.

Between 1801 and 1805, he dropped out of public view completely. Rumour had it that he was living at a Tuscan villa, playing and writing for guitar. Then, in 1805, he got a job with the Princess of Lucca, who was Napoleon's sister, Elisa Baciocchi. He acted as her court violinist for the next eight years; rumours at the time said he was her lover too. In addition to this lucrative post, he went back on the freelance performing circuit from 1809, playing amazing, dazzling works like his *Le Streghe* (*The Witch*). recommended 3 Eventually, in 1813, he made his debut at the famous La Scala opera house in Milan and was a huge success.

Le Streghe, incidentally, was written in 1813. From here on, things seemed to go well for Paganini. He toured Italy, gradually accruing a small fortune until, in 1825, he encountered an unforeseen expense. His name was Achille.

Paganini had been seeing the singer Antonia Bianchi on a regular basis: she was one of the artists with whom he toured. On 23 July 1825, Antonia gave birth to a son, Achille. Although they never married and the relationship eventually fizzled out, from that day, Paganini became a devoted father, providing for his son.

Despite this added expense, Paganini was doing well. And yet, up until this point, he had not toured outside Italy. This was due, in part, to the fact that he was weak and prone to illness – travel at that time could really take its toll on even the healthiest of tourists. In 1827, he took a long rest in Sicily which refreshed and reinvigorated him, and made him determined to see the rest of Europe.

By August 1828, Italy's most famous violinist had launched himself on the global market – he went on tour. Between then and February 1831, armed with his specially-written first violin concerto **recommended 4**, he visited more than 40 European cities in France, Austria, Great Britain, Poland, Germany and Bohemia. Paganini was, it appears, making up for lost time.

Financially, he was on to a winner. His reputation had preceded him by decades and audiences lapped him up. Three concerts in Britain on the 28, 29 and 30 July made him around £800 richer – that's something like £40,000 today. Just as Haydn had done in 1791 and 1793, Paganini made his most money from England and Scotland. Giving a total of 150 concerts here alone, he reportedly made around £10,000 on this leg of the European tour – that's around £500,000 nowadays. It was great money but the schedule no doubt took its toll on the frail composer/performer.

> ## COMPOSERS' NOTES NOTE
>
> ### *Far too many notes, Herr Paganini?*
>
> Paganini's *Moto Perpetuo* (*Perpetual Motion*) involves the fiddler playing some 2,248 notes – which works out as around 13 per second. **recommended 5**

As his tour continued, Paganini became not only richer and richer, but also more and more of a sensation. In Vienna, pictures of him were put on clothes and food. Delicacies were named after him. He would pass people in the street bearing walking sticks and snuffboxes with his face on. This is just the same as merchandising today, only Paganini almost certainly saw none of the profits.

Increasingly, his appearance and his playing were leading to rumours that he was in league with the devil. It's possibly hard for us to understand this now, but in those days it is quite possible that rumours such as those might have been believed. In the end, he was forced to publish a letter from his mother, simply to prove that he did have human parents. In 1828, he lost all his teeth and, together with an already spindly, bowed body due to his childhood illness, he must have cast a rather ghoulish appearance, to say the least. Of course, there are those who say that his public letter from his mother was just another way of keeping the story going and that Paganini benefited financially from the rumours.

Certainly, his concerts had become infamous affairs, not just because of stories but also because of the effect his playing had on his audiences. Following one in particular, around 300 people had to be hospitalised – the official diagnosis being *"over-enchantment"*.

Because he made *so* much money, Paganini has often been accused of being something of a Scrooge, but this doesn't appear to be born out by the facts. He frequently gave concerts for charity and he certainly looked after his son financially. He also commissioned a viola concerto from Berlioz,

COMPOSERS' NOTES NOTE

The devil is in the detail

Sadly for Paganini, the devil myths were set to stay with him beyond the grave. It seems that, just days before he died, he refused the last rights. Ironically, his reason was simply that he firmly believed he wasn't dying. So he turned the priest away. As a result, when the church refused to bury him on consecrated ground, it gave rise again to all manner of rumour as to why he had turned the priest away. He was only buried in consecrated ground in 1876, a full 36 years after his death, following a personal appeal by his son to the pope.

whose music he championed, for which he (eventually) paid the composer 20,000 francs – a generous sum by anyone's reckoning (see Berlioz's Notes for the full story). He also paid some 50,000 Piedmont lire to his friend and lawyer, Luigi Germi, presumably as a gift, although quite why, where and when is a bit of a mystery.

In 1838, despite his vow never to gamble again, he opened a casino in Paris. It was to be a cross between a standard casino and a concert hall. Paganini sank an awful lot of money into the venture – it was called Casino Paganini. But the idea was perhaps before its time. It folded and the composer lost a small fortune, sending him into a spiral of depression and ill health.

Somewhat beaten and a little embittered, he retired, first to Marseilles and then to Nice. His health never recovered, though – a combination of poor spirits and a life of gruelling concert tours had taken its toll. When he died on 27 May 1840, despite his more recent losses on the casino, he left an amazing amount of money to his sisters, his son and his former lover Bianchi. His son was left 80,000 francs alone.

That's Paganini tallied: a very successful, very rich performer and composer. Today, his name lives on not just in his music, which is still considered to contain more or less everything it is humanly possible to play on a violin, but also in various competitions. The Paganini International Violin Competition, for example, seeks out a virtuoso violinist every year and gives out a first prize of around 12,000 euros.

RECOMMENDED LISTENING

 CAPRICE IN A MINOR FROM *24 CAPRICES*
Midori

 RACHMANINOV: VARIATION 18 FROM *RHAPSODY ON A THEME OF PAGANINI*
Mikhail Rudy/Petersburg Philharmonic Orchestra/ Mariss Jansons

 LE STREGHE
Salvatore Accardo/ London Philharmonic Orchestra/Charles Dutoit (some say Salvatore

Accardo is the modern day heir to Paganini and, indeed, he is often lent Paganini's own violin on which to perform his concerts)

VIOLIN CONCERTO NO. 1
Maxim Vengerov/ Israel Philharmonic Orchestra/ Zubin Mehta

MOTO PERPETUO
Gil Shaham/Goran Sollscher

MOSES FANTASY (this is Paganini's reworking of a tune from Rossini's opera Moses in Egypt)
Ilya Gringolts

CANTABILE
Sarah Chang/Charles Abramovich

SAINT-SAËNS' NOTES

Name:	Charles Camille Saint-Saëns
Nationality:	French
Born:	9 October 1835

That's the same year that ... Halley's Comet came round

Died:	16 December 1921

The same year that ... Einstein won the Nobel Prize for Physics

Wealth rating: 💷💷💷

Camille Saint-Saëns was born in Paris, on 9 October 1835. His immediate family were not very well off, despite the fact that his mother came from a slightly more well-to-do background in the Champagne region. Fears for the young Camille's health led to him spending two years of his childhood with foster parents in Corbeil, as well as summering with his mother's relatives in Champagne.

Saint-Saëns musical side showed itself very early, as did a quite amazing intellect. He was said to have had an astonishing love of things which most children of his age considered to be too much like work. He started piano lessons from the age of seven, with a good teacher who had studied with Mendelssohn and, as a result, by the age of ten, he was pretty familiar with a huge volume of Viennese classical music, still pretty much unknown in France at the time. He was also playing Beethoven violin sonatas and, at 13, gave his first recital at the Salle Érard, before going on to the Paris Conservatoire.

At college, even though he didn't win the famous composition prize, the Prix de Rome, he did win other awards which made his name one to be watched. Upon graduation, he took a job as an organist at St Merry in Paris, later moving over to what was considered "la crème de la crème" in the French organ world – L'église de la Madeleine. Both these jobs would have been not only prestigious – the Madeleine job particularly – but also very well paid, and they assured Saint-Saëns financial security. His letter of appointment refers to *"irregular honorariums"* – these were the receipts of fees for weddings and private ceremonies in what was a very fashionable Paris church and, across the year, they could add up to a small fortune.

Despite the extra duties that steady work brought, the financial independence allowed Saint-Saëns to devote more time to composing and very soon – when he was only 18 – his first symphony was performed. Four years later, his second symphony was also heard for the first time.

In 1861, when he was 26, Saint-Saëns began to take on piano pupils at the École Niedermeyer. The composer's own piano-playing technique was said to be phenomenal – he would practise scales with a newspaper open at the piano in front of him. The four years from 1861 is the only period during which Saint-Saëns gave lessons – not for monetary reasons, it's got to be said – and his pupils included a then 16-year-old Gabriel Fauré.

In 1864, having just failed again to win the Prix de Rome composition prize, Saint-Saëns started the first of 12 operas which he was to write across his lifetime. It was not until his third attempt – some 13 years later in 1877 – that he struck opera gold. It was a huge work, a cross between an oratorio and a grand Meyerbeer opera, and based on the story of *Samson and Delilah*. In that same year of 1877, Saint-Saëns received a bequest of 100,000 francs from his friend, Albert Libon, for a requiem. The requiem was to be written upon Libon's death, which occurred the same year. By the following year, the *Messe de Requiem* was complete. Nowadays, it is something of a rarity, while *Samson and Delilah* can be said to be the only Saint-Saëns opera to have stayed in the popular repertoire. **recommended** *1*

By 1877, Saint-Saëns was probably one of the most famous living French composers at the time – in fact, he had by now been given the Legion d'Honneur at the age of just 33: practically unheard of. Throughout the 1860s, he'd had the chance to meet Richard Wagner on several occasions and the two composers had struck up some sort of friendship. Indeed, it is said that Saint-Saëns so impressed Wagner with his amazing piano playing and his ability to read Wagner's scores at sight that he once acted as accompanist while Wagner sang passages from *Das Rheingold* at the Austrian Embassy. By now, Saint-Saëns' third piano concerto had been played by the Leipzig Gewandhaus Orchestra and his violin concerto had been premiered by the great fiddler and composer, Pablo de Sarasate.

When the Franco-Prussian war broke out in 1870, Saint-Saëns gave charity recitals in Paris, but eventually moved to London when the Commune threatened to bring all French life to a standstill. It was here, in 1874 – the year of his *Danse macabre* recommended **2** – at the Crystal Palace that he gave a successful organ recital. Just one year later, he had decided to undertake the first of many lucrative foreign tours, visiting countries such as Russia and Austria.

By the 1870s and 1880s, the Liszt and Wagner schools of composition dominated classical music. Most composers were either Liszt followers – writing traditional Teutonic music, constantly reinvented – or they were Wagner disciples – producing new, shocking, avant-garde music. Saint-Saëns had met and become friendly with the composer Liszt many years before – in the 1850s, in fact – and his admiration and friendship led him to declare his hand as a Lisztean rather than a Wagnerite. His fourth piano concerto confirmed his status in this more traditional circle, as did the music that was to launch itself on the unsuspecting world of classical music in 1886.

The work had been commissioned by our very own Royal Philharmonic Society, and bore a dedication to Liszt himself, who had died the same year. Saint-Saëns would later say: *"In this work, I gave everything I had to give. I will never again write anything like this work."* He was talking about his gigantic Symphony No. 3 in C Minor – the "Organ Symphony". **recommended 3**

Beyond 1886, Saint-Saëns continued to compose and to tour. The following year alone, he played all four of his then existing piano concertos in a single, no doubt mammoth concert in Berlin. Cambridge University awarded him an honorary doctorate of music at what must have been an amazing ceremony in 1893 – receiving honorary degrees the same day were Bruch and Tchaikovsky, as well as the composer and Verdi librettist, Arrigo Boito. Grieg was also given a degree the same day, but wasn't actually present to accept it.

After 1890, Saint-Saëns composed less and less, occupying an increasing amount of his time with foreign travel, in search of the sun. He was a frequent visitor to places which were deemed very much "off the beaten track" for the time – this included the Canary Islands, Saigon and Colombo, as well as Algeria.

In his later years, as he saw his own music become more and more out of place with the music of such modernist composers as Igor Stravinsky, Saint-Saëns turned to music criticism. His opinions became increasingly bad-natured as he saw his own work less and less valued. He did, though, do a lot of important musicological work in his later years, editing the 17th- and 18th-century music of Charpentier.

He died of pneumonia in Algiers on 16 December 1921, whereupon his body was returned to Paris for a full state funeral. This allegedly cost the government of the day 40,000 francs. He was buried in the Montparnasse cemetery. It was now, only after his death, that one of his most lasting compositions could be heard. During his lifetime, he had forbidden its performance – all except one movement – for fear that his serious standing in French music be tarnished. He had written it while on a holiday with family and friends, solely for their amusement, and it featured parodies of composers of the day, as well as famous tunes rewritten in unfamiliar settings. It was, of course, *The Carnival of the Animals.*

RECOMMENDED LISTENING

 "MON COEUR S'OUVRE À TA VOIX"
FROM *SAMSON AND DELILAH*
Jennifer Larmore/Vienna Radio Symphony
Orchestra/Bertrand de Billy

 DANSE MACABRE
CSR Symphony Orchestra/Keith Clarke

 "ORGAN" SYMPHONY
Gaston Litaize/Chicago Symphony Orchestra/
Daniel Barenboim

 CARNIVAL OF THE ANIMALS
The Nash Ensemble/Libor Pešek

 SARABANDE AND RIGAUDON
Tina Gruenberg/London Philharmonic Orchestra/
Geoffrey Simon

RACHMANINOV'S NOTES

Name:	Sergey Vassilievich Rachmaninov
Nationality:	Russian
Born:	1 April 1873

That's the same year that … Buda and Pest combined to form the capital of Hungary

Died:	28 March 1943

The same year that … Rodgers and Hammerstein premiered Oklahoma

Wealth rating: £££££

Sergey Vassilievich Rachmaninov was born into a wealthy and musical family on 1 April 1873. The family lived on a beautiful estate at Oneg, in Novgorod: as a child, Rachmaninov loved nothing more than to spend a few hours running and dreaming in the freshly-mown hay – and then a few more playing the piano.

Rachmaninov was the son of a captain in the Imperial Guards and the descendant of a wealthy noble family. His father, however, frittered away the family fortune early on in Rachmaninov's life and, by the time Sergey was nine years old, the estate was gone and the Rachmaninovs had sold up and moved to St Petersburg. Although this is always painted as a sorry time for Rachmaninov, it did have one overriding benefit: had he continued to grow up as part of the Russian landed gentry, a career in music would almost certainly not have been an option for him. He would probably have been forced into the military, like his musical father before him.

At college in St Petersburg, Rachmaninov was quickly a star pupil. His dour, some would say morose, demeanour leant him a useful air of gravitas, and it may have been this – combined with, at the time, a supreme self-confidence – that led Rachmaninov, the student, to charge five roubles an hour for piano lessons when even the best professors who actually taught the course only charged three.

It was also while still at college that Rachmaninov came to know the grand old man of Russian music at the time, Tchaikovsky. When he graduated, Tchaikovsky was instrumental in getting him an introduction to a good publisher, a man called Karl Gutheil. When Gutheil offered Rachmaninov 500 roubles for his student graduation compositions, I imagine Rachmaninov nearly fell off his piano stool. That translates as around £2,650 today, for the unknown works of an unknown student.

Out of college, things didn't go quite as well. In his lean period after graduation, he was forced to take up various teaching posts, such as at the Mariinsky School for Girls, where his heart was not 100% in his teaching. He also took a job as an accompanist on a concert tour, playing for a violinist who was not really up to Rachmaninov's standard. With much the same attitude he took to teaching, he ditched the tour halfway through, choosing to forego the fee rather than compromise himself musically.

With no regular income, Rachmaninov found himself needing to find a way to pay the bills. *"I found myself out of pocket,"* he said. *"I needed money and I wrote this prelude and sold it to a publisher for what he would give me. I realised, all told, 40 roubles out of it – that is $20 in your money – very little compensation, you will admit, considering the sums the piece has earned the publishers. But, in this case, the law of compensation has worked out nicely and I have no reason to complain."*

He was talking about his Prelude in C sharp minor, the "calling card" piece which he was asked to play, usually as an encore, wherever he went for the rest of his life. ⟨recommended **1**⟩ And just to put both the money and Rachmaninov's words into context, the one-off fee of 40 roubles back then is probably worth about £200 today. Rachmaninov wrote it for a concert at the grand Electrical Exposition in Moscow in the September of that year, and received a further concert fee of 50 roubles – so it raked in a total of 90 roubles.

The C sharp minor prelude was written when Rachmaninov was 19. Three years later came his first symphony, the premiere of which was to go down in music folklore. Despite having laboured for two years on the work, its conductor, the composer Alexander Glazunov, was drunk on the night. The performance was a shambles and was derided as such by the critics. Rachmanimov is said to have hidden backstage during the debacle and he immediately lost not only confidence but his entire creative spark. A conducting job to oversee his own orchestral piece, *The Rock*, in London did little to get him back to normal and in the end it fell to a course of "positive suggestion theory" hypnosis sessions from a Dr Nikolai Dahl to cure him of one of the most famous cases of writer's block in history.

By 1900, the 27-year-old Rachmaninov had completed his second piano concerto, complete with its dedication to Dr Dahl. ⬤ recommended 2 ⬤ His contract with Karl Gutheil was still very much intact and he probably earned 2,000–3,000 roubles for the second piano concerto. The use of the music in the film *Brief Encounter* would bring the Rachamaninov estate a one-off payment of $80,000 in 1945 – equivalent to a fee today of several hundred thousand dollars. But this was of little financial use to Rachmaninov in 1900.

With a reputation that grew with every piece, Rachmaninov knew he had the potential to live comfortably. He never wrote music solely for money, but he did know the value of his music. Eleven songs written in 1901, for example, earned him 3,000 roubles, money that was needed to fund his honeymoon. In his lean moments, he refused to let a need for money dilute his musical ideals. In 1906, despite being particularly short, he gave up the teaching jobs which were his fallback bread and butter.

"I turned in my resignation at the two institutes," he said, in a letter from the time. *"Now I'll have nothing left, either for soul or for the pocket, and the pocket itself is clean as a picked bone!"*

In addition to his publishing, he took up increasing amounts of work as a concert pianist, work which was lucrative but also took a great deal of preparation. Not only was there the venue and repertoire side of things to arrange, but each booking meant huge amounts of practice. Time spent practising was time that couldn't be spent composing, so, again, Rachmaninov often found himself walking a fine line between "making music for money" and "making money for music"

Other sources of money were composition prizes, the biggest of which were the Glinkas, Russian composers' version of the Oscars, set up in the composer Glinka's honour. In 1905, the second concerto won him 500 roubles in the concerto category. In 1906, his cantata *Spring* won him another 500 roubles. Then in 1908, he won his third Glinka, this time for his Symphony No. 2. With it came a prize of 1,000 roubles, which today would translate as around £5,000 today. **recommended 3**

Back then, as now, America was an important territory to conquer for a musician. By this time, America was beginning to hear great things about Sergey Rachmaninov, not least through the published sheet music of his C sharp minor prelude. In 1908, Rachmaninov was faced with an offer of a concert tour of the United States for the following year, and it would be an offer he couldn't refuse: 25 concerts at 1,000 roubles a time. That's the modern-day equivalent of around £5,000 per concert. Of course, he couldn't just play his second piano concerto every time. He needed another concerto, one that would make him show all those Americans just how good he was. So he wrote one – the Piano Concerto No. 3. **recommended 4** Once in America, he was greeted as one of the greatest piano players they had ever heard.

When revolution swept Russia in 1917, the composer left for a tour of Scandinavia, and would never return. In his letters from the time, Rachmaninov claimed to be leaving behind around 120,000 roubles *"bound up in Ivanovka"* but also *"about 30,000 roubles in cash"*. The fees from a short 12-concert tour were enough to keep him going initially, pay off his debts and take stock for a while. He would eventually settle in America, but not before stints in Stockholm, Dresden and, later, in Scandinavia and Switzerland.

In Switzerland, Rachmaninov bought a plot on the shores of Lake Lucerne and set about putting his money to good use by building himself a house. As he put it:

"As yet, I can only dream of the big house, for which a large area has been levelled, just by the cliff, over the lake. I stand here, feast on the view and imagine what beauty there will be in my room through the big window."

No doubt the view of Lake Lucerne from the big window was all the better from the seat of the beautiful new Steinway grand piano, which would eventually arrive soon after, a personal present from Frederick Steinway himself.

Other than the house, Rachmninov's main indulgences were cars and boats. He had been mad about cars for a long time – back in Russia, he must have been one of the first people in his area to get a brand new automobile, which he named *Lorelei*. In his Lake Lucerne period, he bought himself a boat in which to spin round the lake too. On one occasion he asked friends not to tell his wife about a near accident, for fear she would not let him take it out again.

It was around this time that Rachmaninov decided to change careers – from composer/pianist to pianist/composer. This might seem like a rather subtle change, but it meant a huge increase in repertoire, as well as much longer practice periods and a complete overhaul of his neglected piano-playing technique – and less time for composing.

He decided to take a "speculative" trip to America, a trip which very soon paid off. He signed a recording contract with *Edison* – a move which was seen as quite a coup for the Edison Company at the time. He also gained a concerts agent, Charles Ellis. Offers of concert tours were flooding in – 110 dates here, 25 dates here, 52 dates there. He eventually played his first date in the US in Providence, Rhode Island, on 15 December 1918, where he opened with his own transcription of *The Star-Spangled Banner*. A year later, he orchestrated his 1915 work, *Vocalise*, especially for a New York audience. (recommended **5**)

In the years that followed, Rachmaninov spent most of his time touring the USA. By 1921, he considered himself settled there, taking a permanent home looking out across the Hudson River in New York. The concert tours would continue right up until Rachmaninov's death in 1943, just weeks after he had finally been made a US citizen. A statement in one of his letters from 1929 sees him saying *"my net profit for last year was about 9,000 marks"* which, if correct, would work out at around $26,000 today. And that's clear profit! Not bad for a travelling pianist in 1929.

COMPOSERS' NOTES NOTE

King Who?

In November 1938, Rachmaninov was invited by Sir Henry Wood to take part in a special charity concert to raise money for hospital beds for musicians. He was to be the sole soloist in the concert. So important was it to Wood to have Rachmaninov perform that he moved the concert date. This meant that not only did it miss its planned date – which was meant to be St Cecilia's Day – but also that no member of the royal family could attend either. Well, you either get the King of England, or you get the King of the Piano. Wood went for the latter.

By the time he wrote the *Rhapsody on a theme of Paganini* in 1934, Rachmaninov was a very rich man indeed. He wrote it for a particularly punishing year of concerts in which he played 29 dates in America and a further 40 in Europe. recommended 6

Rachmaninov later moved to Los Angeles – to Beverly Hills – where he recreated, to the smallest detail, the home he had left behind in Russia – even down to the type of foods and drinks he kept in the cupboards. Despite still playing successful concerts as late as 1941 and 1942, he became more and more unwell. He died from cancer on 28 March 1943, just a few days short of his 70th birthday. Today, he is one of the highest earning composers in classical music. Thanks to both an explosion of the recording industry *and* an increase in the composer's reputation over the years, Rachmaninov's estate still receives vast amounts from his compositions.

RECOMMENDED LISTENING

 recommended 1
PRELUDE IN C SHARP MINOR
Vladimir Ashkenazy

 recommended 2
PIANO CONCERTO NO. 2
Vladimir Ashkenazy/London Symphony Orchestra/Andre Previn

 recommended 3
SYMPHONY NO. 2
Bolshoi Theatre Orchestra/Evgeni Svetlanov

recommended 4
PIANO CONCERTO NO. 3
Martha Argerich/Berlin Radio Symphony Orchestra/Riccardo Chailly

 recommended 5
VOCALISE
City of Birmingham Symphony Orchestra/Sir Simon Rattle

 recommended 6
RHAPSODY ON A THEME OF PAGANINI
Mikhail Rudy/St Petersburg Philharmonic Orchestra/Mariss Jansons

THE RICH LIST

1. George Gershwin

Anyone who can make $10,000 from just one three-minute song deserves to top any composer rich list.

2. Giuseppe Verdi

A poor start didn't stop this operatic genius from leaving behind millions.

3. Sergey Vassilievich Rachmaninov

Despite selling his C sharp minor prelude for the equivalent of just £200 today, he went on to leave an estate, a house in Switzerland . . . need I say more?

4. Giacomo Meyerbeer

Started rich. Ended even richer. Oh, and was rich in between.

5. Jules Émile Frédéric Massenet

The dark horse of the musico-financial world. Earnings in his last years alone of 700,000 francs guarantee him a high placing on the rich list.

6. Jacques Offenbach

If you can spend 80,000 francs on opera house decorations, you're a rich composer.

7. Gioacchino Rossini

Pesaro peasant, he went on to command astronomical fees and afforded the earliest retirement in music.

8. Franz Joseph Haydn

Poor boy, who ended up living his life in a palace – with a cheque book to match. Even his parrot was worth the equivalent of £35,000.

9. Ridolfo Luigi Boccherini

A comfortable start and pretty-much ever-increasing earnings make Boccherini one of the most successful composers of his day.

10. Niccolò Paganini

Left a whopping amount in his will. Could match The Rolling Stones for earnings "on the road".

11. Antonín Dvořák

Despite impoverished beginnings, he steadily raised his income levels, although not quite making it to the top 10.

12. Jakob Ludwig Felix Mendelssohn-Bartholdy

Started rich and stayed rich. I'm not impressed.

13. George Frideric Handel

A good businessman. The first night of the *Messiah* alone raised £400. The odd bad investment prevents a better position.

14. Franz Liszt

Comfortable start and good occasional earnings. The occasional bad tour prevents him getting higher.

15. Johann Sebastian Bach

From an everyday background, he steadily increased his salary.

16. Charles Camille Saint-Saëns

A useful bequest of 100,000 francs kept him well above the bread line.

17. Peter Ilyich Tchaikovsky

With the help of his patron, he managed to stay financially well.

18. Hector Berlioz

Son of a doctor who always kept the money coming in.

19. Ludwig van Beethoven

A healthy band of patrons and an even healthier appetite for dining out means Beethoven is neither bottom nor top.

20. Edvard Hagerup Grieg

From an everyday background, via government grants, to gracing his countries banknotes.

21. Wolfgang Amadeus Mozart

A surprisingly impressive turnover and not a true pauper's end keep Mozart from the very lower reaches of the composer rich list.

22. Georges Alexandre-César-Léopold Bizet

Despite a downturn during the Siege of Paris, he managed to hold his head above water.

23. Fryderyk Franciszek Chopin

Despite being able to charge 30 francs an hour to more than 150 pupils, a poor start and a poor finish prevent Chopin climbing higher.

24. Achille-Claude Debussy

Not the greatest turnover – very up and down.

25. Antonio Lucio Vivaldi

Born comfortable with a good turnover, but died poor.

26. Franz Peter Schubert

Left only 63 gulden in his will. And had to live with friends.

27. Modest Petrovich Mussorgsky

Rich beginnings and only mediocre earnings mean Mussorgsky stays low.

Edition Peters has been at the centre of the music publishing industry since its first day of trading in 1800 in Leipzig, Germany. It has had close working relationships with many of Europe's most well-known composers, including Grieg, Mahler, Schoenberg and even, in the early days of the company, Beethoven (although, unfortunately, Carl Friedrich Peters declined to publish Beethoven's *Missa Solemnis* because of the composer's non-delivery of a set of military marches).

Today, the Edition Peters catalogue covers the complete range of classical music: from Bach, Beethoven, Mozart, Schubert and Strauss (notably *Also sprach Zarathustra* – famously used in the film *2001: A Space Odyssey*), to some of today's leading composers. The company combines the traditions of more than 200 years of publishing with a thriving publishing and composer promotion programme.

We have four centres of publishing around the world: London, Frankfurt, Leipzig and New York.

For more information about Edition Peters, please visit www.editionpeters.com

LONDON · FRANKFURT/M · LEIPZIG · NEW YORK
www.editionpeters.com